Tall Performance from Short Organizations Through We/Me Power

By

Gary B. Brumback

ISBN: 1-4033-4541-4 (e-book)
ISBN: 1-4033-4542-2 (Paperback)

Library of Congress Control Number: 2002093074

This book is printed on acid free paper.

Printed in the United States of America
Bloomington, IN

1stBooks – rev. 07/05/02

Contents

Preface

We/Me power, the energy from individuals melded into teams that can lead to tall performance, the best kind of performance there is. We/Me power isn't likely to exist in the traditional corporate hierarchy where the workforce is commanded and controlled, not empowered, and who work in functional departments, not cross-functional teams. That's why top-heavy corporations, no longer propped up by forgiving markets and made increasingly obsolete by the Internet that easily penetrates bureaucratic layers and functional departments, will eventually fade into history. As a savvy CEO once said, corporations must change or die, and a prominent business magazine several years ago declared the "hierarchy is dying" and advocated in its place the "horizontal" corporation of self-managed, cross-functional teams.

Tall performance, or the right results not gotten in the wrong ways, is a tough standard to reach and sustain even for empowered teams in shorter organizations, or what I refer to as "lowerarchies." What teams need is a model approach for managing their own performance like the one I introduce for the first time in this book. I call the new approach the "We/Me" model of "MBR." It's "We/Me," because it preserves the power of both individual and team performance without sacrificing one for the other. There could be no teamwork with a "Me" model alone, and a "We" model alone would foster social loafing and drive "MVPs" (most valuable performers) away. It's "MBR," because managing both behaviors and results, not just one or the other, makes a big and practical difference for business success in general and business ethics in particular. MBR is not to be confused with MBO, or management-by-objectives, the classical top-down and results-only approach to managing.

Over the years I have created several versions of MBR, ironically, all for use in tall government bureaucracies, some of the tallest organizations in the world as a matter of fact. One version was considered so innovative that it was showcased to US agencies and their regional offices. Even so, the bureaucracy wasn't built short or for empowered teams, needless to say, and that, plus a slew of silly civil service laws and their implementing regulations kept me from introducing even further innovations. But I'm free from all of that now and so I've totally reengineered MBR and created the new model.

MBR begins with the setting of tall performance expectations and proceeds to the follow-up of those expectations. The follow-up involves tending performance, appraising performance, and sanctioning performance. While these are traditional functions in most any business, they are carried out very differently through the We/Me model because the traditional way gets in the way of tall performance.

One of the unique features of the model is how it allows for full accountability of performance by individuals and their teams through expectations about and the follow-up on both their behaviors and their results. Conventional accountability concentrates on results and ignores behaviors, or the manner in which the results are achieved. By adding accountability for behaviors, important and practical distinctions can be made between positive and negative success and between positive and negative failure. The distinctions may reflect old truths, but these old truths need to have a way of being put into practice.

Another unique feature of the model is the approach to performance appraisal, a subject that has had a dismal history for thousands of years, dating back at least to the fourth century AD in China when an "Imperial Rater" was accused of giving the highest performance ratings to favorites of the Royal Court rather than to the meritorious. Déjà vu! It's no wonder that some critics advocate eliminating the practice altogether. But that's not a viable solution. Tall performance requires performance appraisal because it's necessary for accountability. So, after many years of study and thought I have come up with what I think is a unique, workable, and acceptable solution for individuals and their teams.

The model also departs from the conventional wisdom that in order to preserve teamwork only teams and not also their individual members should be rewarded for deserving performance. That is an untenable proposition, and the model instead provides for both "We" and "Me" rewards for deserving performance.

Yet another unique but also logical and necessary feature is that the model mainstreams ethical considerations into the entire performance management process. It's logical to do so, since ethical behavior is part of tall performance. It's also necessary for doing business ethically and consistently so. The standard corporate ethics program, with its ethics officer, code of ethics, workshops, hotline, and the like, is simply insufficient by itself to foster organization-wide sensitivity to and the practice of ethical business. Obviously, any business desperate and determined enough to stay competitive by breaking laws will do so undeterred by any ethics program, the We/Me model, or existing laws and regulations. But for the rest of the business community, "business ethics" needn't be an "oxymoron." I think the approach introduced in this book can help any business trying to steer an ethical course while not at the same time being outperformed or outlived by the competition.

Because the model is for use by empowered teams, an issue arises that I want to address right now. It's the argument by some that the organization loses necessary control over what's happening if the organization's leader empowers everyone in the organization. But that argument is the old command-and-control mentality associated with layered organizations and also with the concept of management as a position rather than as a process. The model allows for people to control themselves through empowerment that is done responsibly, not irresponsibly.

The book is organized into two parts. The first part gives four guiding principles. Without principles, the new approach could be just another one of those management fads that, for lack of a solid rationale behind it, comes and goes, as so often happens. The second part shows, through the WE/ME model, how the principles can be applied. The model is very flexible. It can be applied to any form of a short organization, large or small, with fewer rather than more management layers. The model also allows empowered people, as they should be allowed, to adapt the model as they see fit as long as they follow the principles and don't repeat the history of performance appraisal.

At the end of the book are some appendices, which I think you'll find very useful if you should decide that the We/Me model or some variation of it is worthy of further consideration for possible use.

I know there are scores of books in which each addresses one or more of the three topics of teams, performance management, and business ethics. So why read and use this book if you are in business, a member of an empowered team, an internal or external consultant, a teacher of business, or anyone who believes in tall performance? I've found the other books to be useful in different ways, but none integrates all three topics into one unique model, the We/Me model, which I think you'll find to be quite promising for its potential in helping empowered teams reach tall performance and stay there.

Gary B. Brumback,
Palm Coast, FL
GBrumback@aol.com

Part One. The Principles Of MBR

Principles aren't like rules. Rules are meant to regulate and are commonplace in bureaucracies and other hierarchies. One of the first things a CEO super leader did after getting rid of his company's many hierarchical levels was to get rid of all its rules. He put it this way, "—most regulations are poppycock—[and] rarely solve problems."[1] You'll learn more about his company later on.

Principles, on the other hand, are meant to explain and guide. They also endure because they reflect enduring truths and ideas. That's why I've so thoroughly grounded in principles the We/Me model of MBR (short for "managing behaviors and results") that I'm introducing in this book. Without principles to support it, the new We/Me model of MBR could become just another one of the dozens of operational fads that come and go among companies world-wide.[2]

There are four principles to explain and guide the use of the new model. The four are introduced in Part One. How they can be practiced in the use of the model is the subject of Part Two. The four principles are these:

1. The principle of the performance equation.
2. The principle of accountability.
3. The principle of empowerment.
4. The principle of performance management.

I have been slowly carving out three of these principles from decades of study, thought, and practice. I have added the principle of empowerment more recently. It would have been out of place in the government bureaucracies where MBR got its start. But the principle of empowerment when applied makes tall performance more likely and thus has been added to help me design the new model.

As you read the principles you may think they're simple-minded, obvious, or old truths. I rather hope you do. There's no particular virtue in complexity, and pointing out the obvious sometimes is necessary when the obvious goes unheeded. So, please now go through Part One and see what you think of the four principles. But I also ask you to withhold final judgment until you see how they're put into action in Part Two.

Gary B. Brumback

Chapter 1. The Principle of the Performance Equation

It's not mathematical at all
And it's the core of every business

The authors of a recent business book make a forceful argument for companies to transform themselves through "creative destruction."[1] I mention the book here because in one of its appendices is a very mathematical equation, a complicated, differential equation at that, which the authors contend helps to portray a company's performance.

My performance equation is not mathematical at all. It's much easier to understand. It portrays not the performance of a company but the performance of each and every person in the company that's at the very core of the company's business performance. So here's my equation for the performance of anyone in business (or in any walk of life) in its most general form:

Personal Traits + Situations   =   Behaviors + Results
(The Inputs to Performance)   (The Outputs of Performance)

Looking at the output side of my equation explains why MBR stands for "managing behaviors and results," not "managing behaviors right" or "managing by results." Both parts of performance must be managed well because it makes a big difference, as we'll see throughout the rest of the book. MBO, or managing by objectives, essentially ignores the first output of the equation.

Let's very briefly examine the general equation and then go on to look more closely at an example of an equation with inputs and outputs very wrong for good business. I'll explain when we get there why it's very important to consider that example.

THE INPUT SIDE

Some disciples of total quality management (TQM) would have us believe that system errors, not human ones, account for most failures.[2] That's simply not the case, although it does fit nicely with the human tendency to take personal credit for successes and to blame the situation for failures. The truth of the matter is that our performance always has two inputs interacting with each other, our own together with those from our situations.

As for what we bring to the equation, each of us has many personal traits. Some are mental (intelligence, for example), some are physical (coordination, for example), some are motivational, (values, for example), and the rest are interpersonal (sociability, for example). Among them, intelligence, or the ability to reason, probably is the most significant personal input to our performance. The old saw that success is 1% inspiration and 99% perspiration is a dull saw. Working smarter cuts through much faster to harder goals. But tall traits besides intelligence obviously can't and shouldn't be discounted. And don't forget short traits like a

3

"sandpaper" personality, for instance. It can negate intelligence in an instant by rubbing people abrasively.

Next, consider the situations we face. They are inevitable because we don't live and work in a vacuum. Situational inputs are any factors other than our own personal traits that also affect our performance. Situational inputs either help or hurt our efforts. I'll argue in Chapter 3 that a tall organization is a situation that shortens the performance of the people in it.

THE OUTPUT SIDE

Fix in your mind the two outputs making up our performance: our behaviors and the results of those behaviors. It's a simple and probably obvious point, but its practical implications are immense, as you'll see throughout the rest of the book.

The First Output-Behaviors

Behaviors are our actions. They can be characterized as tall or short. The tall ones are those behaviors that are competent (both technically and interpersonally), motivated, and ethical and are more likely to lead to expected results. Short behaviors are the opposite yet sometimes yield the expected results. What to think and do about tall behaviors that fail and short behaviors that succeed is taken up in the next chapter and beyond.

There are millions of tall and short behaviors in a lifetime. Our enduring patterns of behaviors over time rather than infrequent or single instances of certain behaviors can be thought of as representing the manner in which we live our lives and pursue our goals.[3]The concept of manner of performance is an ageless, important, and broad one. I'm told that as far back as 2500 BC the Grand Vizier of Egypt wrote a book of instructions on our manner of performance. It's important because it allows for more critical distinctions to be made concerning the nature of success and failure. And it's broad because it encompasses all human behaviors, not just table manners. So whenever I refer to "manner of performance," think far beyond the expensive lessons in etiquette taken by business executives[4] Their companies' money would be much better spent on getting them to help achieve the tall performance their businesses need.

Note in the equation that behaviors are the output closest to the left side. This means that behaviors, metaphorically speaking, are the windows to our hearts and minds. You can't see the traits of intelligence or honesty on the input side, for example, but you can see intelligent and honest behavior on the output side. The distinction between the inputs of traits and the outputs of behaviors is a very practical one. For example, many organizations in their "performance" appraisals mistakenly try to appraise traits instead of behaviors that are caused in part by the traits.

4

The Second Output-Results

Results, almost the sine qua non of business, are the consequences of our behaviors. The results of people at work are either directly in the form of goods and services, or are meant to contribute to them, or to add value to the business in some other way.

It could be argued that results aren't part of our performance because they are physically separated from our behaviors. But that's a specious argument. It's impossible psychologically and economically to separate the two parts of our performance. Indeed, we aim and strive for results, and we're compensated for them.

The basic charter of a business, I believe, is to produce results in the form of goods or services useful to society, to turn a profit, and to do so in a positive manner. Tall results are the ones that do that and more. Short results don't do that. They are of inferior value or worse.

AN EQUATION THAT'S WRONG FOR BUSINESS

I have six reasons for wanting to discuss now a particular equation, that of wrongdoing in business. One, it's hard but not impossible to conduct business ethically, especially in the pressure cooker of competition. Two, championing good business behooves not denying the prevalence of wrongdoing in business. Three; wrongdoing is always harmful; and the harm done sooner or later also envelops the wrongdoer, in this case business. Four, short performance helps to illuminate and give fuller appreciation to tall performance. Five, understanding the nature of wrongdoing even in a simplified way can help guide teams of empowered people in managing their performance, as you'll see in Part Two. Six, it's important to stress that doing business ethically really does provide a positive and different kind of ROE (return on ethics). [5]

When we substitute the wrong elements into the general form of the equation, we get this wrong solution:

Corruptibles + Badvantages	=	Unethical Behaviors + Harmful Results
(Inputs to Wrongdoing)	=	(Outputs of Wrongdoing)

Two General Kinds of Wrongdoing

All wrongdoing is unethical, but there are two general kinds, illegal and legal. This distinction is illustrated in Figure 1.1, and its implications are discussed.

5

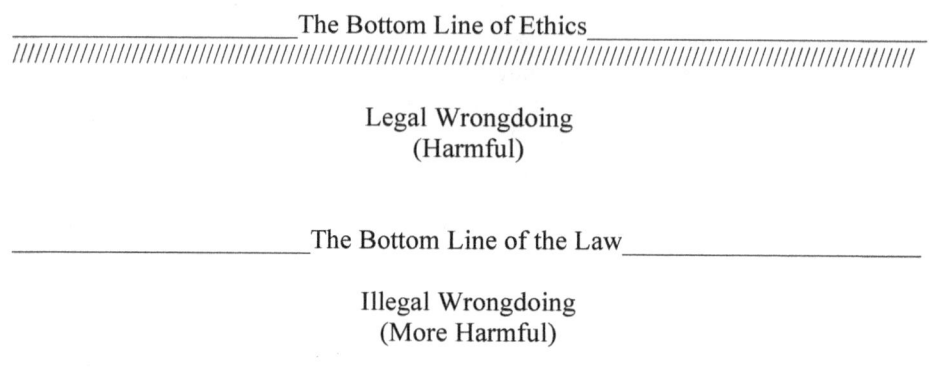

Figure 1.1. The Difference Between Doing Right and Doing Wrong.

- **Everyone should be above the law, way above it!**

Now that's a switch from the familiar admonition that no one is above the law. But I think the unconventional notion makes more sense. As Figure 1.1 illustrates, while our actions may be on the right side of the law, the minimal standard, they may sometimes be on the wrong side of ethics, the higher standard. That we should be way **above** the law is one reason for my metaphor of "tall" performance.

- **The "gray" area of ethics is small.**

The so-called "gray" area of ethics (the striped area) isn't as large as excuse makers, or moral rationalizers, would like to make it. Behaving ethically is less a question of not knowing what to do and more one of not wanting to do it. I think the hard-core ethical dilemmas in life that might perplex even ethicists are rare. Socrates reportedly answered a pupil's question about what is ethical with another question: "Need we anyone to teach us this?" Perhaps not, given that we are mature, civilized adults. But we do need to behave ethically, and behaving ethically is easier said than done.

- **The area of wrongdoing is larger.**

The last time I looked, there were nearly 400,000 web sites devoted to the subject of "corporate crime," and there seems to be headlines of a new and big business scandal every few months with instances in between of lesser infractions. Even so, to put the matter into perspective, there must be millions of businesses world wide, and I'd guess that most, like most of us individually, try to behave legally. Legal wrongdoing, on the other hand, is much more prevalent partly because there are laws meant to thwart illegal behavior. There are no "laws of ethics," though, and my files are bulging with examples of corporate conduct that is on the right side of the law but on the wrong side of ethics. Of course, since we are only human, many more examples could be compiled from all of the other arenas of human life.

- **All wrongdoing is harmful.**

It's taken for granted that illegal wrongdoing causes harm of a psychological, physical, and/or financial nature. That's why we have laws to protect us from ourselves. As for legal wrongdoing, I suppose it might matter only to idealists ("virtue for virtue's sake") if it weren't harmful. But it is. That the harm caused will usually be less serious doesn't turn legal wrongdoing into right doing. Moreover, legal wrongdoing is often a stepping-stone to illegal wrongdoing.

The Behaviors of Wrongdoing

All wrongdoing involves behaviors that breech ethical values. What are those values? The ones found to be common across cultures and time are these: accountability, altruism, excellence, fairness and justice, honesty and integrity, loyalty, promise keeping, respecting others, and responsibility.[6]

Accountability and excellence may seem out of place among the others. Yet, in one source on ethics, the Holy Bible, the idea of accountability is in more than 100 scriptures, and the idea of excellence is in about 75 scriptures. The two values certainly make imminent sense from a business point of view. Tall performance signifies excellence, and accountability is necessary for tall performance.

Another point, obvious or not, that I want to make about the values before moving on is that they shouldn't be used indiscriminately as standards for judging behavior. While the values might seem to sweep across all short behaviors, not all short behaviors are unethical. For example, behaving discourteously stems more from an abrasive personality than from a deliberate breeching of the ethical value of respecting others.

The Results of Wrongdoing

Whatever else may be its results, such as achieving or not achieving some objective, an act of wrongdoing always results in harm to people or property. Consider the case of a lawyer who was a senior partner in the world's largest law firm.[7] He sexually harassed a new secretary. His partners ignored and then rationalized the lawyer's behaviors because he was a big revenue producer. The secretary was emotionally distraught, frightened, and humiliated. That's harm no one should have to endure from the hands of another. So she rightfully sued. The lawyer was forced to resign and ordered to pay $225,000 in punitive damages. The firm was ordered to pay $6.9 million. The dismissal and fines constitute, by the way, what I call "boomerang" harm to the lawyer and his firm.

7

There's another aspect of harmful results. It's the harm caused by services and products often known beforehand to be harmful. Knowingly engaging in such commerce is clearly an act of contemptible wrongdoing and adds immeasurably to what I call the "gross national harm index" that must surely be astronomical. Financial costs alone from such harm have been estimated at over two and one-half trillion dollars annually.[8] As sizable as that is, it's still a gross underestimate of the aggregate harm because it misses numerous other costs as well as all of its psychological harm.

Why Wrongdoing Happens

The left side of the equation explains why wrongdoing happens. "It takes two to wrong do," the "corruptibles" and the "badvantages." Corruptibles are personal traits that predispose a person to wrongdoing. Badvantages are situational factors that tempt or pressure a person to do wrong, thus giving an advantage to bad behaviors.

Wrongdoing happens so easily and is so hard to stop because the left sides of our equations are often tilted in favor of it happening. To illustrate how that is so, I've listed in Table 1.1 some specific corruptibles (C) and some specific badvantages (B). Obviously, I have heavily tilted the list against ethical behavior. But it only takes one corruptible encountering one badvantage to make ethical behavior less likely.

Table 1.1

A Guaranteed Formula for Wrongdoing in Business

In the best and worst of times (B)
Where the conventional bottom line rules (B)
A moral rationalizer (C)
Hurrying to get more (C)
In a tall organization (B)
Occupying a seductive position (B)
Handed down ignoble expectations (B)
With upside-down incentives (B)
And without full accountability (B)

The list certainly isn't exhaustive, but does include some of the more likely inputs to wrongdoing in business, so I want to pause here for a moment to make a few comments about them. I'll also be returning to them occasionally throughout the rest of this book as a reminder that we always need to be on guard against them.

Note that the badvantages dominate the list. Its people, of course, who create almost all of them, and doing so knowingly is itself an act of wrongdoing. If badvantages couldn't be willfully created, thereby leaving only the rare and uncontrollable ones running loose such as widespread economic calamities, wrongdoing couldn't flourish as it does.

<u>The Best and Worst of Times</u>. Needless to say, not only the worst of times, like financial distress, can tilt us toward doing wrong, but the best of times can help to ripen greed.

<u>The Conventional Bottom Line</u>. The overarching badvantage, if you ask me, is the conventional bottom line. You have heard of "publish or perish" in academia. In business it's "profit or perish." I once reviewed for a professional journal a book on "why corporations make good people do bad things."[9] The reason why, the author claims, is the "tyranny" of the conventional bottom line. But it's not inescapable tyranny. Resoluteness to resist and look beyond it can help. I recall a chief executive saying that while he paid attention to his company's quarterly earnings, he certainly wasn't beholden to them. It can also help if the conventional bottom line is tempered by another bottom line. You've already been introduced to part of it. The rest of it is given in the next chapter.

<u>The Moral Rationalizer.</u> With due respect to us all, I think **all** adults are potentially corruptible. Perhaps only saints are at the top of these three broad levels of "morality."

- Unconditional morality "Wrongdoing is wrong, period."
- Conditional morality: "It depends."
- Unprincipled morality: "Do whatever is necessary."

Most of us are probably at the middle level most of the time. It's there where we most need to morally rationalize or excuse our actions considered and/or taken that we know to be wrong. Because we mentally create these rationalizations, I call them "mind over manner," or more aptly, "wrong mind over wrong manner." I've put some short, generic examples in Table 1.2 to remind us of just how commonplace this bad habit is. It's yet another example of where we've met the enemy, and it's us.

Table 1.2

Mind Over Manner: Excuses for Wrongdoing

Denying or trivializing its significance:
"Show me a victim."
"As long as it's legal."
"It's just a technicality."
"You can't legislate morality."
Compartmentalizing it:
"Morality is a personal matter."
"I don't mix business with my personal feelings."
Arguing its necessity:
"It's cutthroat out there."
"It's my job."
"Doing it will save some jobs."
Arguing relativity and universality:
"It's not illegal anywhere else."
"Everyone's doing it."
Professing ignorance:
"I wasn't told."
"Ethics is all a puzzle."
"The rules are inscrutable."

Greed. Greed often underlies the need to rationalize before acting. A sage once poetically said that greed lurks in the hearts of us all. Being not a poet but a psychologist, I would exchange the heart for the mind as the seat of excessively wanting more than we really need. When normal ambition turns the corner and morphs into greed, wrongdoing can't be far behind. It's just waiting for the right-or wrong I should really say-opportunity. But the wait can't be long. Greed isn't known for its patience. We not only want more, we want more now.

Tall Organizations. While the "tyranny" can hang over tall and short organizations alike, the citadel, or "venalyard" of badvantages is the command and control hierarchy. I'll expand on that argument in Chapter 3, but in the meantime, think of where you would most likely find the remaining badvantages on the list.

Seductive Positions. Because of their tempting characteristics, some positions seduce the people in them to do wrong. The most seductive positions are obviously the positions of undiluted or concentrated power. Top management, for instance, is usually responsible for the most serious corporate offenses.[10] There are, of course, many other positions with other tempting characteristics. They include those that require or give incumbents considerable discretion (which is one reason why empowerment needs to be done responsibly and with responsible people), financial responsibilities, obscurity (that is, working out of view), and/or significant dealings with influential outsiders.

Ignoble Expectations. Behind every tall performance is usually a tall expectation, and I'll have much to say about tall expectations throughout this book. Many expectations, on the other hand, aren't tall at all, and some are quite ignoble. Those that are tend to cause people to do ignoble things they wouldn't do otherwise. This is truer where expectations are from superiors, and by "superiors," you know I don't mean people at the highest level of morality. The message goes down the chain of command until it gets to the doers who can't get rid of it without doing its bidding or getting fired. The message may be bluntly direct such as "keep two sets of books" or "squish the competitor like a bug," generally suggestive such as "do whatever is necessary," obliquely given but with a wink and a nod, or implicitly embedded in unreasonably tough objectives. However the message is couched, the expectation is expected to be met or else.

Upside-Down Incentives. One way for management to be more certain that there is follow-through on an ignoble expectation is to tie it to an upside-down incentive so that doing the expected wrong and succeeding gets rewarded and not doing what's expected and failing gets punished. The conventional bottom line clearly wouldn't be so malevolently powerful if it weren't for ignoble expectations and their incentives.

Incomplete Accountability. Being allowed to dodge accountability for unethical behaviors when they succeed, regardless of whether they are explicitly rewarded, obviously gives wrongdoing an open door.

PUTTING TALL PERFORMANCE FIRST

As necessary as it is to acknowledge it, understand it, and to be committed to shun it, I don't want the subject of wrongdoing to end this chapter. Clearly, wrongdoing or any other form of short performance isn't in the long-term best interests of business, but tall performance clearly is. And making some more comments about the best kind of performance is how I want to end this chapter.

To set out for tall performance, the idea of it must be put first in the mind and actions of everyone in business. If a business doesn't put tall performance first, I sincerely believe it eventually will be outperformed and outlived. So there must be a performance culture in the organization in which everyone envisions and values tall performance and puts it as the top priority of the business (see Appendix A for details about a culture of tall performance).

Does the idea of putting tall performance before people seem cold or calculating? I think not. Given what tall performance is, putting it first doesn't mean devaluing and exploiting workers or cutting other ethical corners. Nor does trimming organizational layers have to be done inhumanely. Numerous companies have trimmed layers and done it in very fair and caring ways.[11-12] Furthermore, putting tall performance first is tantamount to putting people first simply because people are the performers. Tall performance is their performance, and you can't get their tall performance without first empowering them.

While the thrust of my book is on explaining why and showing how tall performance can be kept first by letting empowered people manage their own performance and manage it very, very well, there are, of course, many additional ways to help put and keep tall performance and performers first. Business author and professor Jeffrey Pfeffer makes a good logical and empirical case for how a number of additional performers-first practices help improve the conventional bottom line; practices such as selective hiring, and extensive training.[13]

Speaking of the conventional bottom line, I alluded a bit earlier to how its "tyranny" can be moderated by another bottom line. Let's see what I mean by this in the next chapter.

Chapter 2. The Principle of Accountability

The conventional bottom line
Isn't the only bottom line

A major thesis of this book is that tall performance isn't possible in business without accountability not only for the results its people achieve but also for the manner in which those results are achieved.   As I've said, the reason tall performance isn't the norm in business is due in no small measure to the tyranny of the conventional bottom line.

THE BOTTOM LINE OF RESULTS

The bottom line of results, of course, is the conventional form of accountability. Consider in Figure 2.1 conventional accountability for each of two competitive arenas, business in general and the business of big-time sports. The focus and pressure of conventional accountability in those two arenas are on maximizing profits and wins. While their magnitude certainly reflects some behaviors, such as inefficient behaviors, for instance, there is no assurance that there will be an explicit accounting for them, and sometimes there is an assurance that there will be no accounting for illicit but successful behaviors. Conventional accountability is thus incomplete accountability because it doesn't explicitly and fully account for all of our performance.

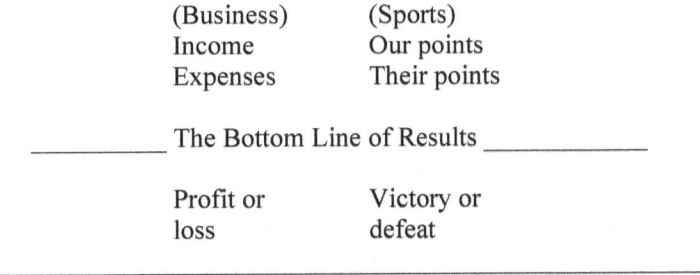

Figure 2.1. Conventional accountability in business and sports.

THE BOTTOM LINE OF BEHAVIORS

The bottom line of behaviors, illustrated in Figure 2.2, is the other part of accountability. Any behavior can be judged as being above or below its bottom line. Such judgments can be made independently of what we think about the results of the behaviors. Knowing right from wrong, for example, enables us to judge the lawyer's sexually harassing behaviors for what they are without having to know their results.

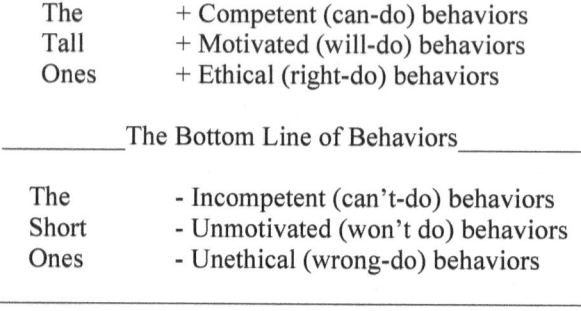

The	+ Competent (can-do) behaviors
Tall	+ Motivated (will-do) behaviors
Ones	+ Ethical (right-do) behaviors

_____The Bottom Line of Behaviors_____

The	- Incompetent (can't-do) behaviors
Short	- Unmotivated (won't do) behaviors
Ones	- Unethical (wrong-do) behaviors

Figure 2.2. The Bottom Line of Behaviors

Our ability to judge behaviors apart from their results makes possible very practical distinctions regarding the nature of success and failure, as you'll see momentarily. But, and this is an important qualification in making the distinctions and in managing performance at work, any single incidence of behavior either above or below the line doesn't necessarily reflect a person's more enduring manner of performance. As I alluded to in the first chapter, a person's manner of performance can be determined much more reliably only by that person's pattern of behaviors over time (of course, a single incident of egregiously negative behavior isn't one to be ignored).

MERGING THE TWO BOTTOM LINES

Behavioral accountability by itself, of course, doesn't make any practical sense. Business isn't in the business of behaviors; not even the theater can thrive on staged behaviors alone. For accountability to be exercised fully and properly, therefore, the two bottom lines must be merged into an unconventional bottom line. I've drawn Figure 2.3 to show how success and failure each have two different meanings when the two bottom lines are merged. The differences aren't just semantic. They are also very practical.

Tall Results Gotten		Tall Results Not Gotten
Positive	Positive	Positive
Manner	Success	Failure

_____The Unconventional Bottom Line_____

Negative	Negative	Negative
Manner	Success	Failure

Figure 2.3. What happens when the separate accountabilities are merged.

Note that the opposite of positive success isn't failure, as would be the case with conventional accountability, but negative success gotten despite incompetent or lazy behavior or because of unethical behavior. Given conventional accountability, these short behaviors are reinforced when they succeed, yet eventually they will spawn negative failures. Successes of the negative kind, therefore, tend to have a short lifespan, and shouldn't be tolerated. Moreover, and this is where the rubber really meets the road so to speak, success gotten unethically should always be penalized.

Given conventional accountability again, this time in penalizing or at least not praising a positive failure, then the positive behaviors that fail because of unforeseen obstacles in the situation may never reappear, and this may foreclose the possibility of such failures eventually turning into positive successes.

Any policy or practice that doesn't reward a positive success or does reward a negative success, along with not penalizing any unethical success, is a badvantageous policy of using an "upside-down incentive."

While the notions of the two different kinds of success and two different kinds of failure may be old truths, rather than a new paradigm per se, I think Figure 2.3 does draw attention more clearly and simply to truths that often go unheeded.

FOUR TRUE STORIES

This is a good place to breathe life into what up to this point has been a rather abstract discussion, even though the truths represented are old and time-tested ones. Here are four stories, two above and two below the unconventional bottom line. The stories are true, but I have decided to keep the people in them anonymous. Two stories are each about a coach. As I've said, sports is big business. But I've also picked these two stories because they so clearly distinguish positive from negative success.

15

The Coach of Sport X-Paragon of Positive Success

His brother called him "the most intensely competitive man I have ever seen," reported the sports magazine that had just picked that competitor as its "Sportsman of the Year." No wonder. He had by then amassed one of the most winning records of any college coach. And the way he did it was even more remarkable. When many in big-time sports stoop below the bottom line of ethics, he has always been above it. In a national TV feature on sleaziness in sports, he told the reporter: "Sure sports is big business, but that doesn't mean it has to be dirty business."

In a championship game that gripped sports fans' attention, his team was pitted against another team that had received a lot of publicity about the misdeeds of some of its players on and off the field. The clean team won.

The Risk Takers-Positive Success the Next Time

With the blessing of the whole organization, an internal team gambled several million dollars in an effort to develop a revolutionary new product. Everyone was committed to the idea and worked hard.

The project flopped, however. Nevertheless, a huge party was thrown for the group. Its director and a few of the members were promoted. Everyone was given expensive gifts. A glowing report was published in the company magazine. A company spokesperson said the celebration was not the case of declaring victory in the face of defeat and withdrawing, but rather a way to encourage people to continue being creative and not to be disappointed when promising ideas don't always work.

The Coach of Sport Y-Extremely Successful, But

His teams won several national championships, including one undefeated season. He ran a clean program, no NCAA violations. He insisted on proper behavior by his players. He insisted on academic achievement, and his players had a very high graduation rate. He raised much money for a university building fund. He was compassionate and caring for his players and others on hard times. But, there was a chink in his otherwise gleaming armor. He had an explosive temper during games and sometimes in confrontations with his superiors. He was finally fired. Many people, myself included, think the dismissal was a bit vindictive and too harsh, yet it would be hard to argue that the coach's temperamental behavior was acceptable.

The CEO-A Case of Ignominy

Three months of journalistic investigations, including interviews with dozens of incumbent and former executives of the imperiled company led to the cover story in a major business magazine pillorying a certain CEO. It told about his belated, forced resignation and explained why.

When he had moved up to be the CEO 10 years earlier, the company was robust and its future bright. But he was corrupted by his newly acquired power.

When he left the company it was debt-ridden and almost belly-up. How he (mis) managed to do that is clear from the pattern of his short behaviors highlighted in the story:

- Started behaving egotistically
- Put sycophants on the board
- Lavished company money on expensive perks
- Accepted unconscionably high compensation
- Refused to diversify when it was the best strategy
- Forced a major relocation despite heavy resistance
- Made costly and erratic investments and divestments
- Favored friends in dealings at company expense
- Refused to admit even his most horrendous mistakes

I don't know whether this poor chap has redeemed himself since. I certainly hope so. Who would want that feature story to dominate one's legacy?

The Moral of the Stories

The moral of the stories is simply this:

- Always strive for positive successes.
- Always accept, maybe even reward, positive failures.
- Never tolerate success or failure of the negative kind.

WHERE THE BUCK STOPS

The immediate results of our behaviors usually are followed by more distant outcomes, sometimes intended, sometimes not. This fact of life raises the question of just how far should the right side of our equations be stretched in exercising total accountability? My rule of thumb is that expectations of performance should take into account the responsibility and authority or influence of the person and past history. For example, the added expectations that a college coach recruit players who graduate and increase revenues for the university may not be an unreasonable one for that particular coach. People tend to expect even more once a string of successes has been produced.

In the following vignette, we see that a wise judge knew how far in a case before him:

> The company was caught dumping over
> 75,000 gallons of carcinogenic chemicals
> into Puget Sound. The judge refused to
> hear the guilty plea of lawyers sent by
> the company. "Bring the company's leader,"
> he ordered, "the public is entitled to know

who is responsible." Three executives were
sent. "No," he said, "I want the top officer
here." Finally, the chairman and the CEO
appeared in court.[1]

In their leadership capacities, these two top executives should have been expected to ensure that toxic wastes were disposed responsibly even though the two never did any of the disposing themselves, naturally.

NOT FOR WIMPS NOR DOUBLE JEOPARDY

One of my hierarchical models of MBR was designed for and used with the Senior Executive Service of the US government in one of its largest agencies. Two senior executives approached me once with diametrically opposed complaints. One of them said, "being held accountable for both manner and results of performance is double jeopardy." In effect, he was whining like a sissy. The other said, "Manner of performance is a wimpy idea." In effect, he was protesting that MBR was for sissies.

No, MBR doesn't put people into "double jeopardy," but does hold people accountable for what they should be held accountable for, nothing more, nothing less. And MBR is hardly wimpy. Wimps aren't tough enough to celebrate positive failures or to avoid negative successes. No wimp is tough enough to do what one executive did, namely, fire a manager of a highly productive unit because of his slave-driving behavior.[2] No wimp could ever match Coach X's performance in an unforgiving business when the going gets tough. And no wimp would do well in an empowering organization, the next principle to which we now turn.

Chapter 3. The Principle of Empowerment

Power can make the organization tall
Or power can make performance tall

WHY EMPOWERMENT?

Empowered people have maximum control over their own performance equations. The equation of an empowered person can be written this way:

PERSON + situation = **PERFORMANCE**

It follows, as you might anticipate, that the equation of an un-empowered person can then be written this way:

person + **SITUATION** = performance

Which one would you prefer for yourself? Self-evident though the importance of empowerment for adult life may be, I nevertheless want to make a case for empowerment by invoking seven imperatives: the biological imperative, the psychological imperative, the ethical imperative, the linguistic imperative, the physics imperative, the philosophical imperative, and the economic imperative. I can't think of a stronger case for this third principle and its practice. Making a strong case for empowerment, furthermore, also makes one for short organizations, because We/Me power is suppressed in tall organizations.

The Biological Imperative

Empowerment isn't only learned. All species are genetically programmed to manage themselves and their own performance. Some start doing so right after birth. Some, like our species, are nurtured and cultivated by adults for a while before being allowed to manage them selves (e.g., drive a car). Any species without this genetically bestowed capability simply could not survive.

Consider birds, for example; they are an incredible species when you think about it.[1] They manage to survive through different seasons. They manage to store food and remember where they stored it. They manage to find a mate. They manage to learn new songs.

Now it stands to reason that since birds can successfully manage themselves around the clock, then mature human beings certainly should be able to do so, too, not just during the time they are away from their workplaces. It's ironic, but mature adults manage their own affairs all of the time, except when at work in un-empowering organizations. I don't mean to suggest that people who work in such places are treated worse than birdbrains, but it's not at all farfetched to say that such organizations are dehumanizing.

Are those organizations most likely to be tall ones? You bet. They're hierarchies with "thinkers" at the top and "doers" at the bottom and in between layer upon layer of managers, with each layer managing the next lower layer. These tall, pyramidal organizations don't empower most of the people in them. People at the highest layers don't distribute their power. Which brings me to an argument I have heard made sometimes, namely, that no one can empower someone else; only each individual can empower himself or herself. I can't buy that argument, not on behalf of most people in a hierarchy anyway. You know what would happen to them if they tried to maximize their own power with all of those layers above them. So even in a lowerarchy, its enlightened super leader must fully share his or her power (you'll meet such a leader later on in this chapter). The principle of empowerment and the empowerment model of MBR described in Part Two only make sense when power is shared.

The Psychological Imperative

Consider the psychology of you. I'm sure you would choose the first of the two equations at the start of this chapter for yourself at work and everywhere else in your life not only because of your genetic predisposition but also because you know the first equation adds to your psychological well-being. Numerous psychologists other than myself have emphasized the undeniable and powerful human nature of empowerment.

Psychologist Carol D. Ryff, for one, specializes in this subject. She makes the very believable case for including autonomy and mastery of the environment in her prescription for psychological well-being in adulthood.[2] Don't you really feel better when you're your own master? I really do.

You may be unfamiliar with Dr. Ryff's research, but I bet you've heard of the psychologist, Dr. Abraham Maslow and his theory on fulfilling human needs and their connection to human motivation.[3] Ironically, it's a hierarchical theory, but in this case, a hierarchy of human needs that conflict with any organizational hierarchy. The first level of human needs is the most basic one, simple survival. When it's met, the need at the next level becomes the most motivating force until it's met and replaced by the next higher-level need. At the fourth level is the need to belong, a need that can be met very nicely by being a member of a team. At the fifth level, the top one, is the need to develop one's potential to the fullest, a need that can be met very nicely through empowered teams where development of multiple skills and compensation progresses horizontally. In a hierarchy, on the other hand, advancement is vertical and more limited. That's one reason why people in it manage their careers more than their performance as they compete for fewer and fewer openings up the pyramid (the other reason as I've already alluded to is that their performance is being managed mostly from above).

Given that he's co-written a bestseller, you may also have heard of psychologist Dr. William C. Byham, if not also read the book, *Zapp! The Lightning of Empowerment.*[4] Small wonder it's a best seller. It joins the ranks of a growing list of popular self-help books, videos, and seminars, all on how to take charge of one's life at work and everywhere else. Occupants of executive suites should take heed of what their people down below are reading. Instead of wasting billions of dollars of their companies' treasure chests every year trying all sorts of superficial ways to motivate their people, corporate leaders would be well advised to undertake two other initiatives instead, flattening their organizations and *zapping* their people into empowered teams.

Then there's psychologist and author Albert Bandura, who gave a keynote address on "Shaping One's Future" at an annual meeting of the American Psychological Society. He has studied and stressed the importance of self-efficacy much of his career. In his address he made the cogent point that "unless people believe they can produce desired effects and forestall undesired ones by their actions, they have little incentive to act or to persevere in the face of difficulties."[5] And who are the people who believe that the strongest? I'm sure it's the empowered people.

The supervisor/subordinate differentiation is at the core of the hierarchy, and it's not at all surprising to me that a decade or more of surveys indicates that more and more *zap* wannabe's don't want to be supervised.[6] Supervisors can no more *zap* their subordinates than puppeteers can unleash and enliven their puppets.

I have been compiling here and there from the literature quotes of people who are *zapped* at work. Here are a few that are a living and working testimony to the importance of this psychological imperative:

> *I'm not a number and don't check my brains*
> *at the door. My judgment is valued. It's terrific*
> *to empower people. We all run the business together,*
> *and it's just had its best year.*
> *Our work is rich in variety and continuously*
> *requires us to learn and grow professionally.*
> *For me, if I never get a promotion, it's still*
> *worth it to work here.*
> *Decisions around here are made more by people*
> *with the right knowledge of what needs to be*
> *done than by people with titles. We don't have*
> *to go through people to get to other people.*
> *We have ready access to all information and*
> *other resources we need to do our work.*
> *I'm expected to judge my own performance.*
> *Given general direction, we have a lot of autonomy*
> *and discretion. We manage our own budget and other*
> *resources.*
> *My workday doesn't drag on; it flies by because*
> *I'm engrossed in what I'm doing.*

The Ethical Imperative

The ethical imperative of empowerment is that its practice upholds these ethical values: altruism, excellence, fairness and justice, respecting others, and responsibility. Altruism, because empowering people is in the best interest of their welfare, including their psychological well being. Excellence, because empowerment liberates potential for tall performance. Fairness and justice, because power is more evenly distributed, not hoarded at the top. Respecting others, because empowerment fulfills the strong need for self-actualization and control over their performance equations. Responsibility, because empowering, not commanding and controlling others, is the responsible thing to do.

Responsibility, by the way, is accountability's helper value, especially in the case of empowerment where people manage themselves. Empowerment doesn't give behavior carte blanche. Empowerment requires responsible behavior by those empowered; otherwise, empowerment could amount to anarchy. Only responsible people willingly accept being held accountable when their performance falls short. That's why it's crucial in an organization of empowered people that they have been selected from among the more responsible and conscientious members of society.

The president of "Three Circles," my name for a real and very short company to be sketched later in this chapter, once said that hierarchies are the "cause of much corporate evils."[7] I agree with him, and for two reasons. One is the unethical premise underlying the rationale of hierarchies that the "doers" are neither smart enough nor enterprising enough to be empowered, are exploitable and dispensable, and only get in some cases less than 400 times the compensation of top executives. The other reason is one I have alluded to in the first two chapters. Hierarchies are a fertile breeding ground for badvantages, such as seductive positions at the top layers, ignoble expectations, and accountability dodges (e.g., the lawyer and his firm and the toxic dumpsters). Given such a premise and a place, is it any wonder that ethics hardly has a fighting chance in hierarchies?

The Linguistic Imperative

What on earth, you might ask, do I mean by this imperative? Well, thinking, talking, and writing, which make up a large part of our millions of lifetime behaviors, depend on language and it can be a very powerful source of power. A Nobel prizewinner in literature, Toni Morrison, has noted an axiom we all know, namely, that words can be used to "sanction ignorance, preserve privilege, and create and perpetuate subjugation."[8]

The language of empowerment definitely isn't the native language found in a hierarchy. Consider the word, "subordinate," for instance. One of its meanings is that of being subservient in an inferior way. Or think of words like "boss," "order," "direct," "superior," "supervisor," "supervise," "lines of authority," "chain of command," and "span of control." Such authoritarian and subjugating terms obviously are out of place in places full of empowered people.

The Physics Imperative

You might ask the same question here. What I mean by this imperative is that Newton's second law of physics tells us that for every action there's an equal reaction. Coupling this law with the psychological imperative and considering the history of labor relations leads me to conclude that for every commanding and controlling action by management there is likely to be a counteraction by those managed. Two British scholars, in researching for their book, *Organizational Misbehaviour*, have conclusively documented how workers, when they perceive they are being exploited by management, counter with work slowdowns, sabotage, and the like.[9] And American psychologist and well-known business consultant Edward Lawler III adds that he's "regularly impressed with the ingenuity of the workforce when it comes to defeating management control systems—."[10] People who are empowered at work, on the other hand, will give a positive outlet to their ingenuity at work rather than waste any energy otherwise spent in resisting management of them by others.

The Philosophical Imperative

If logic isn't to be denied, a philosophical argument needs to be added to the case for empowerment. One of the greatest modern philosophers, Immanuel Kant, regarded the "autonomy of will" as an intrinsic human condition. That is, you may force a person to act, but you can never "will" that person to act. We can only will ourselves. If you accept this as a logical premise, then it also follows logically that being empowered comes much closer to this intrinsic human condition than does being commanded and controlled by others. To Kant, there was nothing "more dreadful" than being subjected to the will of another. I think he would have endorsed the empowered version of the performance equation.

The autonomy of will, incidentally, is also a logical prerequisite for the principle of accountability. Only when the individual wills his or her own actions is personal accountability for those actions logically reasonable.

The Economic Imperative

Money "talks," they say, so let's "listen" to this last imperative. Empowerment that can only be optimized in a lowerarchy is simply good for the conventional bottom line. Two authors in doing research for their book on *Business without Bosses* concluded that there's an immense payoff from using empowered teams.[11] They found such payoffs as 50% or more gains in productivity, 50% or more reductions in manufacturing costs, more work pride and more harmony throughout the organization. Results such as these aren't surprising. As I've said, it's self-evident that empowered people can outperform commanded and controlled people.

The hierarchy, moreover, as an organizational structure per se, simply is not suited for excelling competitively. Decision-making is often constipated when important issues and relevant information must go up and over the different and competing functional silos of the various departments such as R & D, production, marketing, etc. Innovation is stifled because creative ideas from people closest to the real customers must travel up through each level of doubters and deferrers. A hierarchy, in other words, is better as a bureaucracy than as a business.

In their recent book, *The End of Management and the Rise of Organizational Democracy*, the authors tell an interesting story about the CFO of a Fortune 100 company who shortened his organization and instituted self-managing teams.[12] Shortly afterwards, the CFO fell seriously ill and was away for two months. When

23

he was able to return, he was pleasantly surprised and relieved to discover that "critical financial and strategic decisions" had been ably made in his absence. When the results of empowerment can impress a top executive with an eye on the conventional bottom line of a top corporation, I think that's impressive testimony for empowerment.

KEEPING EMPOWERMENT RESPONSIBLE

Given all of its imperatives, empowerment nevertheless comes with a big caveat. Empowering irresponsibly and being empowered without acting responsibly clearly would not be good business and must not be allowed to happen. This concern is why there's the argument by some that the organization loses necessary control over what's happening if the organization's leader empowers everyone in the organization, particularly the large corporation.[13] But that argument is the old command-and-control mentality associated with layered organizations and also with the concept of management as a position rather than as a process. The compelling imperatives for empowerment should educate that mentality.

Hiring responsible people and ensuring that they have or get the skills necessary for the business are the initial safeguards against irresponsibility, but they aren't enough. Having a culture of tall performance is essential, too, but it also isn't enough. As you'll see in Part Two, the entire process of the approach introduced there, including the practice of three "sub principles," are what needs to be added to ensure responsible empowerment. The three are guarded trust, structured flexibility, and partnerships. It's time to meet them here.

Guarded Trust

Guarded trust is somewhere in between distrust on the one hand and unguarded trust on the other. To explain better what I mean, first consider the two extremes.

Distrust is the expectation that the performance wanted will not happen in any but the most controlled situations. It's obviously inconsistent with the principle of empowerment. Below is a true vignette of disgusting distrust by the "leadership" (not worthy of the name in this case) of one very slave-driving company:

> The company installed a new monitoring system.
> The supervisor watches the computer screen,
> which records each worker's output the second
> it is produced. The company was quite pleased
> with the jump in productivity "despite amazing
> levels of demoralization and bad feeling."[14]

It's all guard and no trust at that prison of a workplace. The people there, though, at least knew that they were being hawked. According to a survey of Fortune 500 companies, many of them do not tell their distrusted people that they are being hawked.[15]

Unguarded trust is at the other extreme. It's the expectation that the performance wanted will happen in any situation, regardless. That may not be too risky for the right people in the right situations, but it can be very risky and possibly also a potent badvantage for the wrong people. Recall the case in the last chapter of the unguarded trust the board had in the CEO.

Now consider guarded trust. It's the expectation that tall performance is conditional, and thus there will be times when the process of managing it needs to be strengthened a bit further. For example, it would be prudent for the team to monitor more carefully an inexperienced person who has just joined the team.

Structured Flexibility

I was conceiving the idea of structured flexibility at about the same time Tom Peters and Robert Waterman, Jr. were writing their successful book, *In Search of Excellence*.[16] They observed that the more successful companies they studied exercised rigid control while also insisting on and allowing employees to have autonomy, to exercise entrepreneurship, and to be innovative. They dubbed this practice the "loose-tight principle." But it's much tighter than structured flexibility because the use of rigid controls is inconsistent with the principle of empowerment. Structured flexibility means the right balance between constraints and no constraints on the performance equations of people in organizations (for example, the MB of MBR, or "managing behaviors," does not mean the straight jacketing of people). Just where the balance should be will depend on the circumstances, but it would not be "rigid control." Moreover, as future workforces become more computer literate, they will demand more flexibility commensurate with the boundary-less nature of the knowledge and information age.

Partnerships

Empowered teams and the business, as a whole, can't do well without the concept and use of partnerships within and across teams in the business. A true partnership is synonymous with being a good team. Partnerships are the guardians of trust. When people are partners, they don't behave at odds with each other. Instead, they behave in concert, like members of a great basketball team, for example.

WHAT'S THE FUTURE OF TALL AND SHORT ORGANIZATIONS?

It may be bleak for the tall and bright for the short. Hierarchies got their biggest lift in the United States from the industrial revolution and their biggest rationalization from the theories of Fredrick Winslow Taylor, the "father" of "scientific management."[17] But we are well beyond that revolution, and the theories have long since been discredited. We are well into the era of the knowledge and information revolution accelerated by the computer and its Internet that's quite capable of penetrating the walls of functional silos and leapfrogging over layers. I predict that this new revolution along with the hierarchy's intrinsic deficiencies will eventually seal the tomb of the traditional organizational structure.

Rigor mortis may have already begun. Some years ago, B*usiness Week* magazine declared in one of its cover stories that, "the hierarchy is dying," and advocated in its place the "horizontal" corporation of empowered teams.[18] Many corporations are transforming the way they are organized, and many are using or considering using such teams. An explosive growth in their use is predicted by the authors of *Inside Teams* who cited corroborating findings from several surveys[19] Between 1987 and 1996, for instance, the use of at least some empowered teams jumped from 28% to 78% in the largest public companies.[20]

"Three Circles," Taking Empowerment to its Limit

I want to sketch for you a real business to illustrate how far the empowerment principle can be taken, probably to its limit, and how short an organizational structure can be lowered, probably to its limit. I've descriptively named the company, "Three Circles." The company's real name is Semco S/A, Brazil's largest marine and food processing machinery maker.

When Ricardo Semler, the son of a founder of a moribund company of unionized factories, became its president, he flattened it into three concentric circles, got rid of all the "poppycock rules," maximized empowerment for everyone in the company, and made other radical changes.[21] Not long afterwards, the company became known as a paradise for its members and one of the fastest growing and successful companies in its industry.

The circle in the center, deliberately not labeled the "inner" circle, has a few people called "counselors" (note that there aren't any titles demeaning of others without those titles). The president is one of them (he only signs as "President" on official documents). The people in this center circle integrate the company's operations. The next, larger circle has eight partners, each of whom leads a product-related unit (there aren't any functional departments). The third, largest circle has all of the people in the units. These people are known as associates. They work in teams and do the research, design, manufacturing and marketing work. Associates have no one reporting to them regularly.

Associates who lead team efforts are called coordinators. They are the only ones to whom others in the large circle report, and there are no multiple layering of coordinators. The teams pick their own coordinators. According to the president, if you put ten people together, a leader will eventually emerge. In order to give you an idea of the trust placed in and empowerment given to everyone in this company, I'll close this sketch with three illustrative instances of decision making. In a hierarchy, of course, the bigger decisions are made higher and the smaller decisions are made lower. That can't happen in a flat company. Here is what happens instead.

One of the operating divisions had outgrown its facility. After real estate agents had failed to locate an acceptable replacement, some associates of the division were asked to search for one. They found three factories for sale within days. The entire division was next sent for one day to look at the three, and then asked to vote on a selection. They picked one the counselors didn't like. Now the counselors had a choice, renege on the company's value of a democratic work place, or continue honoring it. The counselors decided not only to let the associates' vote stand, but also to let them design the new layout of the plant once it was bought. About this experience, the president said that the profitable plant really belongs to them and he feels like a guest every time he's there.

In the second example, the president had wanted to buy another company, but associates also outvoted him on that matter. While he wondered afterwards if they had made the wiser decision, he believes the value of democratic decision-making is worth the risk, and adds that it might even have been riskier if a company had been bought which his own associates didn't think would be workable.

The third example is the way pay decisions are made. The limit or epitome of empowerment may be the power to set one's own pay. Everyone at Three Circles has that power, but its use is not irresponsible. Salary surveys are made once or twice a year and distributed to everyone before the next round of pay decisions. Everyone thus knows what everyone else is making for the work they do. They then tell the company what they think they should be paid. Three things can happen as a result of this empowering action. A person can ask for and get the right and fair amount of salary, can ask for and get too little, or can ask for and get too much. For the latter cases, which the president says seldom happens, people are told at the beginning of the next pay setting that the company does not believe they are really earning their higher salary, and that their work will either have to match their pay or they will have to find work elsewhere. Ultimate yet responsible empowerment, therefore, still isn't unconditional.

In concluding this sketch, I want to make two quick observations. First, a lowerarchy, ipso facto, will have fewer or even no people in positions of management. In a lowerarchy management becomes more of a process and less of a position. But no organization, no matter how short, will ever be leaderless. The center circle in Three Circles isn't vacant. In it is a "super leader," one who gets others to lead themselves.[22] Second, note that Three Circles evolved from a unionized hierarchy and stayed unionized. This tells us that unions and lowerarchies aren't necessary incompatible. In doing research for their book, *Empowered Teams*, the authors came to the same conclusion."[23]

Not Going the Limit

My hunch is that Three Circles probably isn't a harbinger of what's ahead, at least in the foreseeable future. The changes made by Ricardo Semler may be too radical for most business leaders. But now that we've seen the limit and how radically different it is from the traditional hierarchy, we can also see that there is plenty of opportunity between the two for less radical changes. Empowerment and the layering of an organizational structure are, after all, matters of degree, with more or less empowerment and fewer or more management layers always possible.

And that's also the way it is with the new We/Me model of MBR introduced in Part Two. I don't want to lose the practical in vainly trying to reach the ideal, so if there are any features of the new model which seem to go to the limit, please bear in mind that those features aren't sacrosanct and that the model can be altered to suit your organization's circumstances. Moreover, in Appendix F I include an overview of the earlier models of MBR that are tradition-bound and not bound to the principle of empowerment. Recall that this principle was added for the new model and isn't necessary for MBR. The other three principles are, however. Take those principles away, and you don't have MBR anymore.

Chapter 4. The Principle of Performance Management

Don't manage people
Manage performance

Unmanaged performance, of course, would be unthinkable, so it's going to be managed one way or the other by somebody or other. MBR is one of those ways. The We/Me are the some bodies. Although its particular form over the last 30 years has varied (see Appendix F), the basic process remains the same, including the new We/Me version. This last principle explains the process, starting with the setting of tall expectations for performance and ending with the sanctioning of performance before the process repeats itself just as the business hopefully does. The process is illustrated in Figure 4.1.

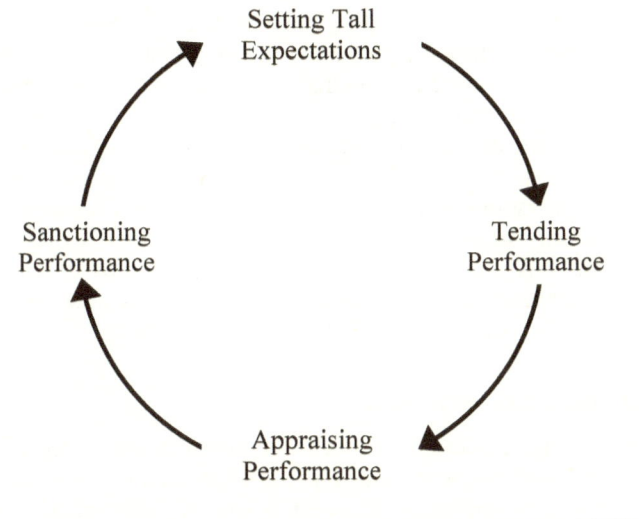

Figure 4.1. The Performance Management Cycle

When there are few or no layers of managers, the idea of management takes on a new meaning. It becomes a process for managing one's own performance rather than a position occupied by someone managing others and giving them orders. Everyone is a performance manager who adds value to the organization's overall performance. No one is a people manager who may or may not be adding any value.

SETTING TALL EXPECTATIONS

Author and business consultant Jon Katzenbach recently wrote a book with the main title, "Peak Performance."[1] That's where the similarity with my book ends. He and I have many different views, starting with what we think peak performance is. He thinks it is performance that's "better than expected." I think differently. I think peak performance *is* the expectation, a tall one to be sure, but still the expectation.

Why tall expectations? They motivate performance. They direct performance. They make accountability for performance possible.

Tall Expectations Motivate Performance

The motivational power of tall expectations has been amply demonstrated through research.[2] But nothing dramatically illustrates this power better than the true story of a Swiss military unit on a training mission in the Alps as told by a wizard on understanding organizations and a former graduate school classmate of mine, Karl Weick.[3] A blizzard hit the unit. For three days the men were hopelessly lost and feared dying. Then one of them happened to find a map in his pocket. Revitalized and elated, they found their way back to the base camp, where they showed the waiting and relieved commander the map that had saved them. Looking at it, the commander was amazed to see that it was a map of the Pyrenees!

What saved the men were their own expectations upon finding the map. Their expectations revitalized them. The map was obviously useless as a guide to give them direction. Any old map would have sufficed in their desperate situation.

The men's expectations were of their own making, not handed down to them from above, as from "higher elevations in an organizational mountain." People obviously will be less committed to an expectation imposed upon them. In a "valley" of self-managed teams, performance expectations arise within the teams and are thus self-made, personally owned, and self-motivating.

Tall Expectations Direct Performance

Expectations of tall performance give direction to the performance that follows. But "any old map" naturally won't do. While the ultimate direction comes from the organization's vision, it obviously will be too general and distant a destination to provide daily or even yearly direction to performance. That's the role of yearly performance expectations.

There needs to be expectations for each of the two different parts of performance, and they need to be made in two very different ways:

> Proscribe short behaviors.
> Prescribe tall results.

I realize that the idea of proscribing short behaviors and the idea of setting tall expectations may seem contradictory, but think of it this way. Empowered people should be allowed considerable flexibility in their choice of behaviors as long as they are tall behaviors because empowerment requires flexibility. Moreover, there's usually more than one tall or right way to achieve the same objective, but there's never a right way that involves short behaviors. In any business dedicated to tall performance, therefore, examples of what are meant by short behaviors at work need to be publicized so that everyone in the organization knows that:

> Behaviors such as these don't
> characterize our way of doing
> business and have no place in
> our business.

Expectations for tall results, in contrast, need to be prescribed and put into written objectives with detailed specifications about exactly what should be expected. Little if any flexibility in the specifications should be allowed under normal circumstances. If a certain quality is expected, for example, then that is what needs to be achieved, and nothing less.

Tall Expectations Make Accountability for Performance Possible

All expectations, of course, whether tall or short, make accountability for performance possible. If nothing were expected of a person's performance, there would be no basis for holding the person accountable for his or her performance. That's the way it is with an infant, for example. Not so for the rest of us.

Expectations thus make accountability possible by serving as the standard against which to appraise and then sanction performance. And although tall expectations by themselves motivate and direct performance and thus may lead to tall performance, there still must be accountability for whatever the performance is. The second principle explained why.

FOLLOWING UP ON PERFORMANCE

Tall expectations without performance might as well be fortune cookies. The fortune is in the tall performance. So there obviously must be follow-through, the performance itself. But there also has to be follow-up, which is different. Follow-up is responding appropriately to the performance itself as it's happening and afterwards.

Following up performance involves tending it, appraising it, and sanctioning it. All of these different types of response are part of the performance management process, all have an element of feedback in them, and all share a common purpose, that of making tall performance more rather than less likely.

Tending Performance

Tending performance has two important functions. The first function is the monitoring of performance and its situations. The feedback from proper monitoring, obviously not the kind of monitoring illustrated in the third chapter, provides useful direction and motivation beyond that provided by the tall expectations. I'm really motivated by seeing, feeling and hearing a good golf shot of mine, for example. The second function is the rescuing of falling performance. Bad shots may send me to the pro for help. But business teams had better be much more knowledgeable and skillful at their business than I am at golf. If they are, rescue efforts should seldom be necessary.

Appraising Performance

We come now to the part of performance management that people usually love to hate, performance appraisal. Its bad reputation is not its fault but stems instead from being so badly misconceived and so badly practiced throughout history (see Chapter 7 for the dismal record).

How should performance appraisal be conceived? It should be thought of simply as a comparison between expected and actual performance, both behaviors and results, and not one or the other as is often the case. How should performance appraisal be practiced? By following the four principles, by not repeating history, and by adopting or adapting the approach illustrated in the We/Me model.

I once debated Dr. W. Edwards Deming, now deceased, who was known as the "father" of total quality management and who hated performance appraisal with a passion, calling it a "sin of management." He argued that it should be abandoned. He argued that it's counter-productive because it creates so much ill will. And he argued that systems cause more failures than people do, making the appraisal of human performance, as opposed to appraisal of system performance, unnecessary.

He was certainly right in calling performance appraisal a sin of management, but his arguments were wrong. It would be impossible to abandon performance appraisal. It's human nature. Just try not making judgments about your own and other peoples' performance. And if you could abandon it, doing so would be both counter-productive and unethical. It would be counter-productive because performance appraisal provides yet more useful feedback. It would be unethical, because performance appraisal is a necessary part of accountability. Moreover, his argument that system failure far out-numbers human failure is simply irrelevant and incorrect.

So abandoning performance appraisal isn't the solution. What we need to do instead is change it from being a "sin of management" to being a simple and acceptable practice for people in self-managed teams where there is no "management" to sin.

Sanctioning Performance

A sanction is any informal or formal reward or penalty in response to performance. Sanctions range from informal, "one-minute" recognition and reprimands to formal rewards and penalties. Formal sanctions ordinarily are the last act of follow-up and are ordinarily based on the performance appraisal. However, they obviously need to be timely. Whenever egregious wrongdoing happens, for example, sanctioning it should hardly be put on hold until a year-end appraisal is made.

While sanctions provide still further feedback about performance, they have two more important functions, especially when they are formalized and also are meaningfully significant to the performer. One is to motivate future performance. That is, the prospect of being formally sanctioned significantly and meaningfully is intended to serve as an incentive for tall performance and as a disincentive for short performance. Sometimes, though, sanctions have an effect opposite to the one intended, as in the case of a reward that is insultingly too little and too late. And sometimes they do what they are meant to do, but badvantageously, as in bribes for wrongdoing and other upside-down incentives. So sanctioning should be done responsibly.

The other more important function is that of accountability. Formal sanctions in response to both parts of performance finalize accountability for it. Penalties are more commonly associated with accountability, but as we know, accountability also has its positive side. For instance, when you think you deserve to get and then you do get a formal reward for your tall performance, in effect you wanted to be and then have been held accountable for that performance.

Sanctions need to be linked, not locked, to performance. Locking prevents the flexibility often necessary in deciding upon a particular sanction. For example, if there is a rule (which you won't find in Part Two but can find, for example, in a rigid "table of penalties" in a rigid hierarchy) that a formal reprimand is required for one offense and dismissal required for the same offense repeated five times, any mitigating circumstances could not be considered. The linkage obviously can't be too loose, though, or decisions may be arbitrarily and capriciously made.

We have now covered all the principles. But we're not through with them. If we were ever through with them, why have them? In Part Two coming up, I'll show how people in self-managed teams can use the principles to manage their performance and manage it very well.

Part Two.   Putting The Principles To Work: The New We/Me Model Of MBR

Part Two takes you through my newest model of MBR. I call it the We/Me model because it blends individualism with teamwork. In doing so, it offers a very practical solution to a dilemma said to be tough enough to "stump the most seasoned executives," namely, how to "marry individualism with the importance of working together toward the same goals."[1] A "Me" model alone would destroy teamwork. A "We" model alone would encourage social loafing among any would-be slackers and, worse still, would drive away the "MVPs" (most valuable performers).

SETTING THE STAGE

The model is so new that it hasn't been tested or used anywhere yet. In order to illustrate it in an organizational context, therefore, I'll need to put it into a company of empowered people. So I'll simply invent one, a hypothetical manufacturing company.

Let's imagine the following about my hypothetical company. It shortened itself a few years ago. It has established a culture in which tall performance is envisioned and valued. The company has a super leader as its president. It has counselors (for example, financial counselor, legal counselor). And it has thousands of other members who are all organized into empowered teams (from now on I'll refer to these empowered teams simply as teams). The teams are already established, having been built during a carefully planned implementation stage to get them up and running.[2-5] Each team chooses from among its members a leader or spokesperson, a "secretary/treasurer," and usually a performance consultant, all three of whom serve in those roles for however long the team decides.

It has a Steering Counsel (the president, the counselors, and team representatives) that sets the general direction of the company, charters each team at its inception, allocates company resources among the teams, helps to ensure that their activities are coordinated and aligned with the company's vision, values, and strategic goals (see Appendix A) and adjudicates disputes when necessary.

It has a Performance Review Board (PRB) made up of team representatives with certain responsibilities relating to the appraising and sanctioning of performance (described in the last two chapters).

When it hires new people it hires the right people the right way. I've written elsewhere how that can be done.[6] Opportunities are provided for people to learn and to be compensated for multiple skills needed in the business.

Because many decisions are made throughout the entire performance management process, I've included in Appendix E a list of "conscience-checking questions" and other suggestions on how to make good decisions. And because decisions always involve making choices, and making choices usually involves conflict, I've also included some suggestions on how to make conflict workable.

This isn't the place to go into the details of planning for and implementing a successful transformation of a hierarchy into a more empowering, team-based, shorter organization (Appendix A does offer some suggestions on getting started). Consultants on the subject of organizational transformation abound, and books and how-to manuals have been written on the matter[7].

THE FLEXIBILITY OF THE MODEL AND MBR IN GENERAL

Since it's a model, it's meant only to give empowered teams a general framework and some suggestions, not rules, for carrying out MBR. You'll note as you continue that I rarely say, "must." The principles are more important than either the model or my suggestions (including any "should's") for how to practice it. Thus, empowered people are entirely free and even obligated to manage their performance however they choose given the vision and value of tall performance, but I hope they would at least hew faithfully to the four principles and also avoid the many follies in the long history of performance appraisal (see Chapter 7).

As you read through the remaining chapters, which follow the performance management cycle, please keep in mind that the model absolutely doesn't depend on a real company being like my hypothetical one. It could just as easily have been a non-manufacturing company, for instance. Or it could be very large or very small as long as there are fewer rather than more layers of management. Moreover, whether real companies with a similar structure (such as a Steering Council and PRBs) emerge in the foreseeable future doesn't really matter as far as the model is concerned. Its flexibility is constrained only by its principles. Moreover, and as I've already mentioned, empowerment is a relative matter. It can be increased or decreased on several of its dimensions, including those of decision-making authority, control over resources, structured flexibility, guarded trust, and partnerships. Organizational layering is also relative, ranging from none to (way too) many layers. The model, therefore, can be adapted to any kind of organization that leans toward more rather than less empowerment. There doesn't even have to be self-managed teams for the We/Me model to work. Teams and even traditional work groups can be supervised by front-line managers, as long there is some degree of empowerment and some mix of the We/Me aspects of performance management.

The best evidence for the flexibility of MBR in general is the fact that other models of it have been used by some of the world's tallest and highly structured bureaucracies (see Appendix F). One model used by senior executives and subordinate managers, for example was widely acclaimed, and I was asked to showcase it around the country. An experimental model with a few features similar to the newest model (minus empowered teams, and some other features) was successfully tested in a pilot study for the US government. However, that model was never implemented because it would have required the US Congress to eliminate some of the requirements in its civil service laws (e.g. a requirement that ratings must be used in performance appraisal). It would have been easier to move a mountain. But my effort was very much worthwhile, nevertheless, for it was a positive failure that motivated me to design the We/Me model to be described next.

Chapter 5. Setting Tall Expectations

WHAT THE PRINCIPLES ADVISE DOING

- Responsibly empower the setting of tall expectations.
- Proscribe short behaviors.
- Prescribe tall results.

Setting expectations is so commonplace that it would be hard for people not to do so whether in business or in life generally. Setting tall expectations isn't commonplace, however, yet it's <u>the</u> most crucial requirement for managing performance well because it's the starting point. Poor starts don't augur well for good finishes.

PROSCRIBING SHORT BEHAVIORS

As I mentioned in Chapter 4, examples of what are meant by short behaviors at work need to be publicized so that there is an understanding throughout the organization about what kinds of behaviors are being proscribed. Before implementing MBR, therefore, the Steering Council should appoint an ad hoc team to create examples to put into a handbook. I have already done a good bit of the team's work for it. In Appendix C are some suggestions on how examples can be created, publicized, and used. Many examples are also provided that could be included in the handbook with little or no alteration.

Having such a handbook available is much better than having a typical code of conduct, which is usually full of legal abstractions and not incorporated into the performance management process. Furthermore, companies that have codes don't operate above the bottom line of law anymore than do companies without them[1]

PRESCRIBING TALL RESULTS

Tall results are or relate to the business of goods and services that are of superior value, beneficial to one or more groups of stakeholders (e.g., customers) and intentionally harmful to no one. Prescribing tall results makes it perfectly clear exactly what results are to be expected. The prescriptions are written down in the form of tall objectives. Unlike the list of short behaviors done only once, new objectives obviously must be set for each new performance year.

Tall objectives must have all of the characteristics shown in Table 5.1 (see Appendix B for the details). I've seen many not-so-tall objectives that missed one or more of those characteristics. That's not taking good care of business.

Table 5.1

-Tall Objectives-

- Are Self-Owned
- Are Correctly Aligned
- Are Responsive
- Are Ethical and Environmentally Responsible
- Are Clear and Specific
- Are Change-oriented and Changeable
- Are Quality Oriented
- May Also Target Quantity, Cost, and Timeliness
- Are Track Able and Appraisable
- Are Tough but Doable.

If the company sees that it may be leapfrogged by the competition, even tougher, taller objectives may need to be set and scaled. I call them "Alpine" objectives. They stretch the doable into the maybe by targeting quantum changes that usually require revolutionary new work processes. Such objectives thus tend to court positive failures, as in the case of the risk takers I told you about in the second chapter. Yet Alpine objectives can be very inspirational and aren't always futile. In one reported case, for instance, an objective to improve quality one hundred-fold in just four years was met.[2]

The best place for Alpine objectives is in a place where teams own their work processes and can rethink and redesign them whenever necessary. Even so, the effort will usually be a risk, but one nevertheless worth taking if seen as necessary and carefully planned and executed.

SETTING TALL OBJECTIVES ILLUSTRATED

What follows now is an illustrated process for the setting of tall and even taller Alpine objectives in my hypothetical company. The process has five steps, but they can be modified in number and nature to suit the organization as long as the spirit of the We/Me model is upheld:

1. Teams start thinking ahead.
2. The Steering Council considers teams' initial inputs.
3. Teams draft their "We" objectives.
4. The Steering Council considers teams' drafts.
5. Team members develop their "Me" objectives.

Step 1. Teams Start Thinking Ahead

The teams don't wait for the next performance year for direction from above. There is no "above," no waiting for the cascading down of increasingly narrower objectives as in the case of the traditional, hierarchical MBO, or management-by-objectives. Moreover, the teams aren't in the dark. They know all about the company's vision, strategic goals, and past and present performance, including financial status, because they have been actively involved in all aspects of the company's business. Also unlike a hierarchy, teams can see the connection between their objectives and the overall goals of the company.

All teams, through their representatives, are to suggest at the first of two upcoming Council meetings ideas for what the company's new annual goals should be and what initiatives the teams might take to help accomplish those goals (initiatives that receive concurrence by the Council will then be transformed by the teams into objectives). A new annual plan for the company will then be drafted as a result of that meeting.

To prepare for the first meeting, each team should meet to start thinking ahead. It does this by raising and answering among themselves such questions as: "Do we think our company's current vision and strategic plan are still viable? How well did the company and we as a team do this year? Is there any carry-over work to be done? What do we think are the future prospects for the economy and for the company's standing in the marketplace? What do we think our competitors will be doing? What other situational factors do we need to consider? What products need to be improved? What new products are needed? Given our answers to these questions, what do we think should be the company's new goals, and what should be our initiatives in support of them that fit into our areas of accountability (these areas broadly delineate the results for which each team will be responsible such as, for example, certain products and any associated processes like engineering, manufacturing, packaging, sales, and service)?"

If any truly Alpine initiatives were to be considered, a harder look would need to be taken at two sets of situational factors, dependencies and contingencies. Dependencies are the work processes that will be used and the resources that will be needed to carry out any initiative. The resources may be people (e.g., the Council, other teams, suppliers), financial, information (e.g., marketing data), or things (e.g., equipment). Contingencies are the uncertainties in business life that can stop an initiative in its tracks if they happen (e.g., the competition could surprisingly take to market sooner the same new product under development). Ignoring these crucial factors would very likely doom success, and in ignoring them would also turn failure from positive to negative since the team's planning would have been faulty.

Step 2. The Steering Council Considers Teams' Initial Inputs

Several items should be on the Council's agenda. Among them would be a few ongoing matters to be revisited for either reaffirmation or revision. For instance, the values, vision, and strategic mission of the company should be revisited (see Appendix A for an empowered way to arrive at a vision and set of values in the first place), as also should be the list of short behaviors and the teams' accountability areas.

The primary agenda item would be to choose tentatively the company's new operating goals and the teams' supportive initiatives for the new year and to put them and a summary of the proceedings into a draft plan for the new year. Questions much like the foregoing that each team addressed would be raised and answered. Eventually, the company's new goals and the teams' supportive initiatives would be established. The meeting would then adjourn.

Step 3. Teams Draft Their "We" Objectives

Each team should now begin drafting a set of team objectives and a plan of action for accomplishing each objective. The team objectives must come from the supportive initiatives and must be tall ones (that is, they must possess all of the characteristics in the checklist of Table 6.1). The plan of action includes milestones for critical tasks necessary to be performed and process maps where appropriate.

An Example of a "We" Objective. Lets' consider as an example a team objective that calls for producing a prototype of a revolutionary new product. The objective would be an Alpine one. The prototype has never been designed before. Radical retooling would be required. And the criteria in the objective are very demanding. Here's what such an objective might look like:

"To produce by date W the prototype that successfully passes
a test production run and meets all quality specifications with
a cost not to exceed X amount."

Embodied in this objective are track able and appraisable conditions for three criteria, amount, timeliness, and cost. The fourth criterion, quality, would be contained in an attachment to the draft objective (see Appendix B). Also attached to each team objective would be a plan of action. Usually it should be a brief and general map for getting from start to finish on the objective (remember the Alps story). However, checkpoints or milestones along the way for tracking progress on each would be noted. The plan for each objective should also include any applicable dependencies and contingencies and corresponding courses of action that would need to be taken to secure the necessary resources and to respond to any of the identified contingencies that may arise.

All objectives should be checked against the checklist of characteristics for tall objectives before the teams' representatives go to the second Council meeting. There should also be no question that any Alpine objectives deserve that designation.

If There's a Need to Query Customers First. More than the usual feedback from customers may be advisable before embarking on new initiatives, especially any Alpine ones. Teams ordinarily have at least two sets of customers, the first buyers (e.g. dealers) and the final users of the company's products. Users are by far the more important buyers because if they don't buy, the company ceases to exist. Nevertheless, first buyers such as dealers can't be overlooked because their perspectives can be somewhat different (e.g., dealers' expectations about the company's warranty support). Both sets of customers should be considered active partners with the company in decisions relating to product changes.

Questionnaire surveys are one way to query customers about the company's products and plans. Another more innovative and in-depth way is an approach called "Backwards from Perfect" by its advocates and "Forward to Perfect" by me.[3] A group of some 20 prospective users, a local dealer, and a few supplier representatives, for instance, are selected for "focus-group" discussions (so-called because the group focuses their discussions on a particular subject). One of the company's team's members serves as the group's facilitator and starts the meeting with a very general description of, let's say, a new product the team is considering making. The group is first asked to imagine a perfect model of the product and then asked a series of questions intended to yield a more specific description of it. Most of the questions focus on the eight dimensions of quality listed in Appendix B. The group depicts what it imagines to be an ideal for each of the eight (the group can then be asked if desired to "work backwards" to a perhaps more realistic model). The meeting is adjourned following the group's recommendation to go ahead or not go ahead with the initiative (the team should decide whether additional market research should be done).

Step 4. The Steering Council Considers Teams' Drafts

All teams' draft objectives and action plans would be reviewed and discussed at this second meeting. Assuming teams had communicated among themselves beforehand when concerned about possible redundancies and conflicts among objectives and possible dependencies on each other, no objectives should have to be changed (for example, a team could secure a tentative agreement from another team to exchange two members whose expertise would supplement the receiving teams). And basically because of that, neither would any changes have to be made in the annual goals.

Next, measures of overall company performance on all of the goals would be chosen (e.g., X percent reduction in product recalls, X percent increase in market share, etc.).

A final draft of the annual plan would then be ratified. It would still be treated as a draft throughout the year because it's important not only to plan ahead for change, but also to be prepared to change plans along the way if necessary. The meeting would then be adjourned.

Step 5. Team Members Develop Their "Me" Objectives

Now it's time to move from the "We" to the "Me." Team objectives differ from individual members' objectives in several respects. Because their accomplishment contributes to company goals, team objectives are broader than are individual objectives (the accomplishment of which, in turn, must contribute to the team objectives). Because they are broader and because there are fewer teams than individuals in the organization, team objectives will be outnumbered by individual objectives. Finally, most if not all team objectives will target end results in the form of products to be delivered or services to be provided, whereas most individual objectives will target intermediate or enabling results such as process improvement outcomes or components of the product or service that contribute to the end result (even so, responsibility for such results is a much greater responsibility than lowly doers have in the bowels of a bureaucracy). This final distinction is as obvious as it is critical. If most or all team objectives were process-oriented, for example, the team would be substituting busyness for business. And process, being neither a service nor product, does not bring home the bacon.

Clarifying Roles and Responsibilities. Before members set their own objectives, the team should do a quick review of everyone's roles and responsibilities. The process is different from an analysis of positions. Positions would be totally incongruous and dysfunctional in our mythical company. A position would be like a prison in which narrowly skilled inmates do programmed work details, whereas a role would be like a repertory theater in which multi-skilled actors may need to rotate among different parts and plays from one performance period to the next.

The process the team uses could be a short and simple round-table discussion in which members take turns suggesting in general terms what their own objectives should be in order to contribute to the team's objectives. An individual's objectives, of course, need to be ones that the person has the skills to do. As the discussion draws to a close, the team facilitator would draw a matrix of rows and columns to show the proposed roles and responsibilities. The row headings are the members' names. The column headings are the team objectives. The matrix would be reviewed, any necessary adjustments made, and then approved by the group.

An Example of a "Me" Objective. With their roles and responsibilities in mind, the members would now draft their individual objectives and action plans. One of the team member's objectives might say this:

"To reengineer the process at no more than cost X and by
date Y for trouble-free completion of the prototype."

The team would then meet to review the draft objectives and action plans and to designate at least one if not more of the Me objectives as connected directly to any Alpine objective of the team. The latter, objective, needless to say, isn't going to be accomplished by itself. Some of the team members at least will have to work on it.

Following the review and the making of any necessary changes, the draft objectives and plans would be ratified.

The process I have just described for setting tall objectives would take a few days. During that time, other critical activities would not come to a standstill. For instance, there may need to be last-minute work in finishing work on some objectives from the previous or outgoing performance year. Whatever the case, once everyone has their new objectives in place, they are ready to leap into action to achieve those objectives.

Chapter 6. Tending Performance

WHAT THE PRINCIPLES ADVISE DOING

- Responsibly empower the tending of performance.
- Monitor performance and it situations.
- Rescue performance if it's falling.

Tending performance, it will be recalled, means monitoring it and its situations and rescuing falling performance if it can be rescued.

MONITORING PERFORMANCE AND ITS SITUATIONS

Note that the "P" factor of the equation isn't included in the heading of this section. That's because, as I've already said, personal traits like intelligence or conscientiousness can only be "seen" through behaviors. People, per se, aren't really the objects of monitoring, therefore. Only their performance and the situations surrounding it can be monitored.

While three-fourths of the performance equation is still a lot to be monitored, it ought to be and can be done in a practical way. And it certainly needs to be done in a principled way. Recall the example of unprincipled monitoring in the prison of a workplace I cited in the third chapter. Here are a few more examples I have gleaned from the media. Hiring professional spies to monitor the workplace. Reading all employees' e-mail after promising that all messages would be confidential. Monitoring employees' keystrokes. Bugging offices and rest rooms. Eavesdropping on telephone calls. Call-accounting. Hidden long-distance cameras. Video-spying through peepholes. Rifling through desks and mail. Requiring excessive cash-outs at cash register lines. Telling employees that refusal to accept intrusive watch dogging by the employer is grounds for dismissal.

Such heavy-handed monitoring is imposed on millions of employees daily by distrustful management in command and control organizations in efforts to boost productivity, reduce employee wrongdoing against the employer, and protect against potential claims of negligent hiring. Legitimate ends, yes, but they do not justify the means, which may be legally permissible in most circumstances, yet violate one or more ethical values, are wasteful, and usually backfire.

Principled monitoring, on the other hand, helps to ensure that tall expectations will be met. The most valuable function of monitoring is that of feedback about the performance as it occurs. Think of the initial setting of tall performance expectations and of the subsequent feedback received by the performer as giving a one-two punch respectively to short performance. Expectations motivate and guide performance before the performance begins. Feedback motivates and guides performance after it has started and continues to motivate and guide it until those tall expectations are met.

Monitoring Behaviors

Recall those millions of our lifetime behaviors, many of them while we are at work. I roughly estimate over 30,000 of them from each individual each day at work. Monitoring that many behaviors by people not doing the performing would be the antithesis of empowerment and impractical and ridiculous, whether with the naked eye or through electronic surveillance. It would be all watching and no working for the watchers.

For a practical approach to monitoring behaviors that would be consistent with responsible empowerment, following a common-sense guide like the following is suggested:

Short Behaviors?

<u>No and None Likely</u>   <u>Yes or Likely</u>

Self-Monitoring   Team Monitoring

Self-monitoring should be sufficient under most circumstances where short behaviors are less likely to occur and also where performance appraisal requires minimal if any documentation of behaviors during the performance year. Research, by the way, has shown the superiority of self-feedback from self-monitoring over feedback from others' monitoring.[1] While there are advocates of one-minute praises and reprimands from managers during the course of performance, such a practice certainly contradicts responsible empowerment and, I personally think, is both insulting and patronizing because it treats adults as if they were children.

But formal team monitoring may be necessary if short behaviors become a problem or are likely to become one (e.g., in the case of a new and inexperienced team member). The examples of short behaviors in the company's handbook (see Appendix C) will help to sensitize team members to the kinds of behaviors needing attention if they occur during the performance year.

Monitoring Results

Monitoring results involves keeping tabs on progress toward meeting objectives. Progress means that results are evolving as they should, and if they continue to do so, then the objectives will be met. Monitoring results requires keeping informed about any factors that might adversely affect progress. This includes monitoring situational factors and behaviors. It also includes monitoring the process and schedule specified in the action plan to ensure that the right steps are taken at the right times. As for whether the right results are evolving, the objectives themselves determine what must also be monitored. Consider the team objective described in the previous chapter:

> To produce by date W the
> prototype that successfully
> passes a test production run
> and meets all quality
> specifications with a cost
> not to exceed X amount.

In this objective are the ultimate indicators (e.g., cost) that will tell whether the expected results for this objective have been achieved. These indicators will help determine the performance appraisal, but cannot help in providing feedback and guidance along the way. Intermediate indicators are needed to do that. Not having the ongoing information these indicators provide would be tantamount to "driving a car without a dashboard," as author and consultant Christopher Meyer has put it.[2] He has put his metaphor into practice by helping organizations to design computerized, dashboard-like formats with "colorful graphic indicators and other easy to read gauges" for the team to monitor. He believes they are user-friendlier than are the more popular spreadsheets. There should be a gauge for each intermediate indicator of the result expected (e.g., tracking the schedule with a gauge showing number or percentage of interim milestones reached) as well as for all relevant factors that can be put into this format (e.g., tracking resources with one or more gauges showing the status of suppliers' deliveries).

The dashboard analogy, of course, is not perfect. Not everything needing monitored can be gauged, among them badvantages and contingencies. Additionally, the feedback from a gauge can sometimes be too late. Obviously, when any team member sees a critical problem looming or happening, then is the time to take corrective action.

Monitoring Situations

Teams need to be constantly on guard against any signs of situations beginning to change for the worse, such as a possible downturn of the economy, a possible upturn of a competitor, a possible shift of consumer interest, a possible shortfall by a supplier, a possible breakdown of equipment, and so on and so on.

Self-monitoring alone is too risky when it comes to monitoring situations. People aren't omniscient. They don't have eyes in the back of their heads. Team members need to help each other to monitor the dependencies and contingencies identified earlier and to be alert for any possible or actual changes in them. Each category of dependencies and contingencies, such as internal resources, work and team processes, external resources, market trends, the competition, technology, governmental regulations, and the like could be formally assigned to one or more team members to monitor (but with the reminder that everyone is responsible for staying attuned to possible changes within these categories) and to report back to the team. Other teams and the Steering Council also need to be alerted on any situational matters relevant to their interests and to the organization as a whole.

Monitoring the competition raises the question of just how far to go with that activity. My answer is to go as far as possible while staying ethical. An example of how far to go before stopping is the common practice of benchmarking a competitor's product by buying it and doing reverse engineering on it to see how it was built. I believe that's a perfectly ethical practice (although I think more creativity and less imitation in product development and improvement would be a far better way to gain competitive advantage). An example of going too far would be industrial espionage, such as bugging a competitor's headquarters.

There's another situational category to keep all eyes on, the possibility of badvantages. While they are much more likely in a hierarchy, ethics can't be taken for granted anywhere. To augment alertness to any possible badvantages, the Steering Council should periodically have a questionnaire survey done that asks members their perceptions of any conditions that may favor unethical behavior (see Appendix A).

RESCUING FALLING PERFORMANCE

Performance is falling whenever any troublesome short behaviors occur and/or there's a risk of one or more objectives not being met. The notion of rescuing falling performance suggests that any short behaviors and/or situations dragging performance down are known, that a rescue is possible, and that the rescue can be done quickly. If a rescue isn't possible, positive or negative failure needs to be declared and a decision on what to do next needs to be made.

I'm not going to dwell on this topic for three good reasons. First, and as I have already mentioned, if responsible and capable people manage their performance well, that is, if they adhere to the four principles and practice the We/Me model or some variation of it, then short behaviors should be a rarity. Second, when they do happen and rescue is possible, the topic goes well beyond the scope of this book. There are just too many possible short behaviors, too many possible situational obstacles, and too many possible interventions to be dealt with comprehensively here. Three, quite frankly, the topic also goes well beyond my limited expertise. I would have to lean on others. And that's also precisely what empowered teams should do, lean on their "performance consultants" who have been chosen and trained to take on the extra, helper roles of mentors, coaches, and resource guides.

So all I can do is make a few suggestions here and also in Appendix D for teams and their performance consultants that I feel comfortable about making.

Feedback-The Quickest Rescue Possible

I have chosen the term "rescue" because it calls for quick action. The two most common responses to falling performance aren't quick at all. They are procrastination and paralysis by analysis. Teams can avoid them by using immediate feedback, and then, if that fails, intervening with quick troubleshooting (if knowing the cause of the trouble would expedite the rescue and the cause isn't immediately obvious), followed by correction of the problem.

The most immediate feedback, of course, is "Me" feedback, like holding up a mirror to oneself. This self-feedback is inevitable and instantaneous, and as I've already said, it's often the superior feedback. When I hit a bad golf shot, for instance, I immediately know that it's bad, and so I make adjustments for the next time.

But I'm hardly a good golfer, so my adjustments are often trial and error, with error always making up a large part of my score. Self-feedback, therefore, isn't always superior or infallible, and when it isn't, "We" feedback from others, such as from a team member, will be necessary. "We" feedback without any further intervention than someone else holding up a second mirror and pointing out what is happening may be enough to get performance back on track if the problem isn't too difficult or serious.

Suppose, for example, that a person forgets the second step in a quality check procedure and is about to go onto the next step. If a team member notices the omission, simply pointing it out may be all that's necessary for the second step to get done in time.

Or suppose a person has begun to pressure unduly a good supplier to cut costs. A team member who's aware of this ill-advised and possibly unethical behavior, instead of reprimanding the person, could simply point out the possible consequences if the action continues, such as losing the supplier, and suggest an alternative course of action.

If feedback from others continues to be needed and/or if additional intervention is required because of short behaviors that have become a problem, then those behaviors, feedback and other efforts should be documented and held by the team's secretary or recorder so the information can be retrieved for reference later when needed, such as in appraising and sanctioning performance.

Time-Out for "Feed Forward"

There may be instances when "feed forward" outside the team is needed. In the case of serious wrongdoing, for instance, anyone who knows of it should be expected to report it (e.g., to the PRB or Steering Council). Or in the case of a shortfall that could adversely impact another team, it needs to be alerted, obviously.

A report of serious wrongdoing should document the behaviors that occurred, state when they occurred and under what circumstances (as a way of possibly helping to explain why the behaviors occurred and of determining any mitigating factors), relate if necessary the behaviors to examples of proscribed behaviors in the handbook (see Appendix C) and, finally, describe any tangible harm done. This information ought to be enough to learn, from the perspective of the reporter, what happened and possibly why it happened, and to begin thinking about what course of action would be appropriate. If punishment is the action under consideration, due process should be made available to the alleged offender before a final decision on a punitive action is made (discussed further in the last chapter).

Feed forward about serious wrongdoing raises two issues I want to discuss here, what stance to take on whistle blowing and whether the whistleblower's identity should be disclosed.

The disparaging view of whistle blowing is that it's an act of betrayal. But in a business that puts a premium on tall performance, including the upholding of ethical values, anyone knowing about serious wrongdoing, even if it benefits the business (in the short run), should be expected to report it. Moreover, failing to do so could itself be considered an ethical transgression. Therefore, it should be made perfectly clear that anyone who knows of serious wrongdoing by any one in the business is expected to report it immediately.

The prevailing practice regarding disclosure is to accept and act on anonymous reports. The argument for anonymity is that disclosure inhibits reporting negative information about someone else for fear of acrimony or retaliation. The argument against anonymity is that it can foster irresponsible reporting and also prevent holding the reporter accountable for the report if it's fallacious. I lean toward disclosure, but appreciate the issue and, in any case, the decision ought to be up to the empowered people in the company to decide how to handle this issue.

When Simple Feedback Isn't Enough

If feedback fails but the fallen performance isn't beyond reach, any performance consultant, other team members, and definitely the person not performing up to expectations, need to discuss the matter. That person needs to participate in the discussion not only because he or she is still empowered, albeit a bit less so at the moment, but also because learner-centered learning is far better than teacher-centered teaching. The latter forces the person into a passive role and doesn't address the person's unique needs.

Unless the cause of the problem is obvious to those concerned, quick troubleshooting will be necessary in order to guide the choice of a solution. When focusing on short behaviors, it should usually but not always be readily apparent which of the three kinds they are. However, that won't always be the case when trying to differentiate between incompetent and unmotivated behaviors, and knowing the difference will obviously guide what's done next. For instance, it may not be immediately clear whether working slowly is caused by a knowledge or skill deficiency, a motivational deficiency, a situational problem, and/or a personal problem. In such a case, it's useful to turn to the left side of the performance equation and raise questions such as these:

- New technology?
- Necessary training not given?
- Unclear performance expectations?
- Unrealistic performance expectations?
- Same work done well before?
- Same or similar work recognized when done well before?
- Personal problems?

If the short behaviors are the wrong do's, and presuming the badvantages have been eliminated by design, then such questions as these are appropriate:

- Grudge against the team or company?
- Overly ambitious?
- Rationalizer?
- Financially stressed?

The point of the questions isn't that they should be asked of the person being given the feedback, and indeed the personal ones should not be for they're an invasion of privacy. The point instead is that answers are often visible to team members if they first think about the questions.

Once the nature of the problem is clear, the choice of an appropriate intervention ought to be relatively straightforward in many cases, particularly with a performance consultant on hand. For instance, if the trouble is determined to be a minor skill deficiency that will take a bit more effort to remedy beyond immediate feedback, then help from a mentor or coach for the duration of the performance period should be sufficient. If the skill deficiency is more serious and could jeopardize meeting a team objective, then the team may have to take over some of the person's work and complete it. If the problem involves serious won't do or wrong do behaviors, then a penalty may be in order and possibly not delayed until after the performance appraisal at the end of the year (see Chapter 8).

Returning to the skill deficiency, and it will have to be returned to until the matter is closed, the choice of what to do further might not be so straightforward, aside from the performance appraisal and sanctions at the end of the performance year. More coaching? Classroom instruction? Computer assisted learning? Critical-thinking exercises? Operational manuals? Behavior modification? Performance-improvement plan? Accelerated learning? Different responsibilities? The team along with the skill-deficient person should consult with their performance consultant before proceeding any further, but I deliberately tossed into the options three that come with my definite opinions about them.

Classroom instruction? Think twice about it. Expensive. Slow. Teacher-centered. At best, this classical but not outmoded form of intervention could give the person more knowledge and maybe also some improved skill in applying the knowledge, but applying what's been learned back in the business is unlikely to happen.

Behavior modification, or BMod? Don't even think once about it. At first blush it would seem to be tailor made for the "B" of MBR. BMod is a carrot and stick approach for replacing unwanted behaviors with wanted behaviors. But both its premise and its practice are very questionable. The premise is that behavior can be modified through manipulating its immediate consequences, namely, rewards and penalties. The performance equation tells us that rewards and penalties aren't the immediate consequences. But that's a conceptual argument. My practical argument is that BMod's practice is paradoxical, patronizing, and counter to MBR; paradoxical, because the scheduling of rewards and penalties is randomized while at the same time the importance of immediate sanctions is being stressed; patronizing, because adults are treated as if they were children or pets undergoing socialization or domestication; and counter to everything I have said so far and will say later about sanctions, including not one word about randomly giving them, which is silly psychology.

Performance-improvement plan, or PIP? With a PIP, the person usually signs an agreement acknowledging a performance problem and agrees to take specific steps within a certain time period to improve performance. Some degree of documentation is advisable for use in performance appraisal (discussed in the next chapter), and PIPs are one way to document the problem, the intervention planned, and the outcome. If PIPs are used, never let them become "Frozen PIPs," which is exactly what I have called them in their use in the bureaucracy. Frozen PIPs there went on interminably despite a specific timetable and were essentially cradle-to-grave havens for the marginally performing.

As for anything further on what to do about rescuing performance, I have added Appendix D for the in-house performance consultants. There they will find my suggestions for some further readings on the matter, mostly of the self-help type.

Chapter 7. Appraising Performance

WHAT THE PRINCIPLES ADVISE DOING

- Responsibly empower appraisals.
- Appraise both behaviors and results.
- Appraise performance against expectations.

AND WHAT HISTORY TELLS US NOT TO DO

Performance appraisal is a traditional specialty within my field of industrial/organizational psychology, and for some masochistic reason I gravitated toward it early. I thus know performance appraisal like the back of my hand. It seems like I have lived with both about as long. It may sound like bragging, but you'll see instead that it becomes in a moment a contrite confession. From early graduate school days forward, I have read about performance appraisal, researched performance appraisal, written about performance appraisal in many venues, and have given invited addresses and many other talks about performance appraisal. I have even created and dressed up as "Capt. Appraisal" on stage to take audiences on a time capsule tour of the subject. Able to establish rapport with the audiences, I knew I was on to something, probably their deep-seated distaste for a matter they would just as soon deep-six. And you? What's your reaction to performance appraisal? You must have one. Everyone's got a reaction, and so did our ancestors, and their ancestors, ad infinitum.

So when I say the history of performance appraisal is strewn with foolish practices, please believe me, I should know. Sad to confess, I have contributed my share to them. Since we don't want to repeat them, bear with me for a moment while I become Capt. Appraisal on paper to highlight only the more imitated or outrageous practices. In doing so, I shall try to be as brief and lighthearted as possible because the history is long and the subject can get heavy.

The Search for Foolproof Ratings

You're undoubtedly familiar with rating scales, commonly used by supervisors to rate their subordinates' performance. For far too long I advocated, researched, and developed performance-rating techniques, not only because clients required them but also because I foolishly believed in them. But that's history for me now.

One of the persistent shortcomings of performance ratings is that they are usually several shades from the truth. Dishonest ratings have been a curse for nearly two millennia if not longer. The Emperor of the Wei dynasty in the fourth century AD appointed an "Imperial Rater" to rate the performance of official family members. One of the members rated, Sin Yu (how fitting a name), protested that the highest ratings were given to favorites rather than to the meritorious.

Now back into the time capsule to the late 20th century. A manager in the audience arose after one of my talks to say that he wasn't about to give honest ratings anymore because it penalized his subordinates when his agency gave out performance rewards. Deja vu! And in one agency so many executives were given ratings of "outstanding" that the only executives who stood out were those with lower ratings!

Organizations tend to go from one popular fad to another searching for a way to foil modern-day Imperial Raters. What is found and used each time never works and usually makes the organizations using the newest fad look foolish in the eyes of appraisers and the appraised alike. Are you familiar with any of the following fool-no-one practices?

Rubber Band Rating Scales. Rating scales are quite vulnerable to and actually invite fudged ratings, with the fudging usually being on the upward side, from, say, a "four" to a "five" (there are at least two conspirators when upward fudging occurs, the supervisor who knowingly fudges and the subordinate who knowingly accepts it). Since the difference between a "four" and a "five" could be anyone's guess, a counter tactic that fools no one is the stretching of the rating scale every few years or so by the organization in a futile effort to stay one step ahead of its supervisors (e.g., five rating levels are stretched to 10 and eventually to 50 and on to 100). Supervisors don't fall for the trick and keep on fudging and rationalizing about it.

Forcing Raters. Since supervisors keep on fudging, easily seeing the rubber band for what it is, another tactic used by the organization is to get more sly or more tough with them.

One sly and diabolical technique that has perhaps come the closest in history to being foolproof is known as the "forced-choice checklist." It was invented where I went to school. Not only was I spoon-fed on it in school, soon after, with growing doubts about the technique, I arrived in one of my early career jobs only to find out that it had been implemented in the organization by my superior for enforced use with highly educated professionals (physicians, dentists, engineers, etc.). For years I couldn't escape it. It's called "forced-choice" because supervisors must choose from among quadruplets of illustrative incidents of performance those that will represent their ratings. The trick is that while all of the incidents in a set look equally good or bad, only one is supposedly a real marker for good or bad performance. Supervisors hate the technique because of its deviousness and because it is so complicated to use and to explain. Subordinates don't like it either. I would be surprised if it is still used anywhere. It epitomizes performance appraisal technology run amok.

A less subtle kind of forced rating tactic is what I call the "cracked-bell technique." It forces supervisors to spread their ratings along a bell curve (e.g., using a five-level scale, no more than two percent of the supervisor's subordinates could be rated at the highest level). The bell curve, of course, has nothing to do with actual performance. Moreover, the bell curve assumes random hiring and no training, hardly a reality in any sane business.

Rater Police. In this approach, higher-level superiors police subordinate ratings made by their own subordinates and penalize the supervisors judged to be out of line in their ratings. But on what basis are the "superior" judgments made? Superiors usually aren't as close to performance one or more lower levels removed.

Circular Ratings. Another tactic very popular today is known as "360' Feedback," in which raters below, around, and above the person rate his or her performance. One rationale for this laborious tactic is that the fudging by multiple raters will cancel each other out. But what happens instead may very well be "group fudge." Moreover, where would a lowerarchy get any raters above and below the person rated?

Stumbling Around Ratings. A way around ratings, of course, is not to use them. What I call "person to person," "creative writing," and "counting and clocking" are examples of this practice.

In "person to person," supervisors compare each subordinate's performance with that of the other subordinates and then rank the subordinates from best to worst. That's really an incomprehensible thing to do, though, since a person's performance should only be compared against the performance expected of that person.

In "creative writing," supervisors are given basically a blank sheet of paper on which to write narrative evaluations. But these narratives reflect the supervisors' literary skills more than their subordinates' performance.

"Counting and clocking" is an effort to minimize subjective appraisals by limiting them to performance that can be measured. Believe it or not, once I saw in use a performance standards for one rating level that read, "Attends two professional meetings a year," and the standard for the next higher level was, "Three professional meetings." To be sure, "count" is in "accountability." But that doesn't mean that everything countable or clock-able is worth appraising or measuring. Conversely, not everything worth appraising is countable or clock-able. This is especially true of the behavioral part of performance, and within it most particularly, the ethical dimension. While behaviors can be counted to some extent, it would be silly and wasteful to count them (with some possible exceptions, such as documenting incidents of egregious behaviors in order to justify an intended firing).

Other Follies

Not all follies stem from the desire to stem manipulative raters. Here are some other follies not to be repeated.

Paperless Appraisals. With the advent of the computer has come the fad to automate ratings. Yes, it sounds efficient. But it is "gigo," garbage in, garbage out. Paperwork can best be taken out of performance appraisal by making paper work for you, not against you. Performance appraisal is far too important to let it be taken over by any computer. Performance appraisal, and the rest of the performance management process ought to be a hands-on matter.

Trait Appraisals. This diehard habit dates back at least to the biblical period and shows no sign of stopping. The bible's authors seemed to have been obsessed with judgments, which are tantamount to appraisals ("performance appraisal" is not mentioned in the bible). I found in the King James Bible that twice as many judgments were made about traits (e.g., "meekness") than about performance (e.g., "deed"). Traits, of course, are on the left side of the performance equation and can't be appraised per se.

Anniversary Appraisals. This refers to the annual scheduling of appraisals on employees' hiring anniversaries in order to spread the administrative workload over the year. But an organization doesn't operate the rest of its business on everyone's anniversary, so performance appraisal doesn't have a chance of being meaningfully integrated into the business cycle or the rest of the performance management process.

Isolated Appraisals. Performance appraisal, even when it coincides with the business cycle, often has been neither connected to planning on the front end nor to consequences on the back end of the performance management process, thus becoming nothing more than paperwork. I imagine you know or can guess what happens if performance ratings are disconnected from sanctions-a lot of the fudging goes away. But, of course, one of the purposes of appraisal also goes away, namely, accountability.

Appraisal Immunity. This practice allows the dodging of accountability either partially or fully and it comes in at least four forms, each with its own rationale.

The first form is most relevant here because it occurs when people work in teams. It can be practiced in two opposite ways, with the first being actually practiced now and then and the second being more conceptual. They are "We, not Me" and "Me, not We." In the first way, the team but not individual members is appraised and rewarded. The rationale is that this practice fosters teamwork by not pitting individuals against each other and that it's difficult to determine the individual contributions of the members. The second way is just the opposite, with the rationale being that teams don't literally perform; only its members do.

A second form of appraisal immunity is "topless" appraisal, where executives don't get performance appraisals and "bottomless" appraisal where blue-collar workers don't get them. In each case again, there's a rationale for each practice ("executives are measured against the bottom line;" "blue-collars against a production standard").

A third form is the "presumptive" appraisal where only those to be given the lowest or highest ratings are appraised in order to justify some penalty or reward.

A fourth form involves cases where only results are appraised for certain people (e.g., those responsible for measurable outcomes) and in other cases where only behaviors are appraised (e.g., for staff people with "softer" jobs).

Appraisal immunity and the dodging of accountability violate several of the principles and simply can't be good performance management. Of the four forms of immunity, I want to underscore emphatically the fallacy of the "We, Not Me" appraisal practice, and what usually accompanies it, team rewards but not individual rewards. The practice doesn't allow for individual accountability, which is essential. The practice glosses over the fact that since each member has individual objectives, then each member's performance, both behaviors and results, can be appraised. And by not connecting rewards to individual performance, several costly consequences are guaranteed; stars, or most valuable performers (MVPs), will eventually leave in disgust, slackers will get a free ride, and dissension is sown throughout the team.

Ethics-Blind Appraisals. I have found very few examples of performance appraisal in which ethics was an appraisal consideration, with the US government possibly setting the worst example of where ethics is deliberately kept apart from appraisals of its civil servants. Its argument for excluding unethical behavior from performance appraisal is that conduct and performance are not the same. This policy has created two confusing administrative and legal tracks for dealing with "poor performance" versus "misconduct," and also anomalous cases like the one in which a government executive was caught picking Uncle Sam's pocket, but given a favorable appraisal at the same time! [1] The policy is dead wrong. The very meaning of conduct is behavioral, and thus includes all behaviors, including the ethical and unethical ones. This logic seems clear and convincing enough, but I tried and failed to get the administration and the US Congress to change their regulations and laws on the matter.

Multiple-Purpose Appraisals. There is the belief that performance appraisal has too many purposes and that some of them force supervisors to play conflicting roles such as judge, coach, and pay master simultaneously. This belief has led to some foolish and wasteful practices such as holding separate appraisal-based discussions between supervisor and subordinate for different purposes or, worse still, having different appraisals made for different purposes.

Six Lessons Learned

So much for history. What are its useful lessons for us? In general, don't repeat it! And, as I have already argued, performance appraisal should not be abandoned. It needs to be done, and done the right way. Moreover, if it is done the wrong way, it may end up being overturned in a court of law. In particular, there are six lessons that need to be underscored.

First, performance appraisal, like many approaches to management, is very faddish. Organizations often go from one new approach to the next because they aren't guided by sound principles.

Second, no one should be vaccinated for performance appraisal. Immunity violates several principles and can't be good performance management.

Third, performance and its appraisal shouldn't be shortchanged by including only what can be measured.

Fourth, and related to the third lesson, performance appraisal should include considerations of whether performance has been ethical. There is no better way to sensitize people to the organization's proscription of wrongdoing than having them know that consideration of ethics is part of the appraisal and the consequences it triggers. Ethics training can't do it alone, nor can codes of conduct that are often overly general, too legalistic, or out of sight and out of mind. A group of middle managers once claimed they knew nothing about the company's ethics policies, having forgotten that they had signed copies of the policies "as a condition of employment!"[2] The handbook of short behaviors, on the other hand, isn't likely to be forgotten.

Fifth, performance ratings are badvantageous vehicles for dishonest fudging by manipulative supervisory raters with not-so-hidden agendas. Thus, a business invites unethical behavior among its people if it uses performance ratings.

Sixth, performance appraisal needs to be kept simple. Complexity is not necessary, and unnecessary complexity is counterproductive. Remember, too, that performance appraisal is only one part of performance management. To reiterate a point, tall expectations are more important and deserve more attention.

STICKING TO PRINCIPLES-BREAKING AWAY FROM HISTORY

Not long ago, a member of our professional society wrote in its journal that "we desperately need to rethink this whole area (of performance appraisal), and we need new approaches—."[3] She knows its dismal history, too.

So I'm introducing a new approach here. It's a natural outgrowth of the principles, a different and simple way to appraise performance that's consistent with the principles, very inconsistent with history, and part of the We/Me model of MBR.

The two most fundamental features of the approach are the use of questions to appraise performance and self-appraisal. Using questions instead of ratings eliminates fudged ratings, ipso facto. Using self-appraisers is a hallmark of empowerment. But it's empowerment made responsible through the exercise of guarded trust, partnerships, and structured flexibility.

I'll illustrate the new approach with five steps that could be followed. Again, though, the number and nature of the steps aren't as important as adhering to the principles and avoiding the mistakes of the past.

1. Guidelines are created.
2. Team members self-appraise own performance.
3. Team members get two reviews of their manner of performance.
4. Teams review/certify members' appraisals and self-appraise team performance.
5. The PRB resolves any disputed members' appraisals and reviews/certifies all team appraisals.

Step 1. Guidelines are created.

Flexible guidelines, not inflexible rules nor even their cousin, policies, are useful to have and follow whenever a reasonable degree of uniformity in behavior is desired. Since everyone in the organization should do performance appraisals roughly the same way in the interest of fairness, guidelines to be followed that are consistent with the principles should be created. Having the Steering Council or the PRB lay out some steps to be followed like I'm doing here should provide such uniformity.

Step 2. Team members self-appraise own performance.

Each team member separately appraises his or her own performance by answering a series of questions like the ones I have listed next:

The "Me" Appraisal Questions

A1. How many objectives?
A2. All met?
A3. Which one (s), if any, were clearly exceeded, and what were the extra gains?
A4. Which, if any, objectives more closely tied to which company goals?
A5. Significant contribution to any Alpine objective (s)?
A6. If yes, briefly describe contribution.
A7. Any unexpected and very tough obstacles encountered?
A8. If yes, which objective (s) involved and, briefly, what were they?
B1. Anything (else) special about your performance?
B2. If yes, briefly describe.
C1. Manner of performance consistently positive (see Appendix C)?
C2. If not, briefly describe what happened if not already documented.
D1. A team member and someone else who can review your manner of performance?
D2. Two people whose manner of performance you know well?
E1. Nominate anyone as an MVP?
E2. If yes, who and briefly explain why.
F1. Any performance skills you need/want developed?
F2. If yes, identify and briefly explain what and why.
G1. Data insufficient on results/Any answers difficult to verify?
G2. If yes, identify and briefly explain what and why.

Certain of these questions are needed to determine if any deserving team members should get larger performance rewards (coming up in the last chapter). Take two members, for instance, where both had a consistently positive manner of performance (C1) and both met all their objectives (A2). If that were the only information available, then the two individuals should share equally in any reward. But if one member has more favorable answers to certain other questions (A1, A3-7, B1-2) and perhaps was also nominated as an MVP, then that person should be considered for a larger reward.

There is another reason for including questions B1-2. They are intended to appraise and account for performance when it's impossible or unnecessary to plan for all possibilities. For instance, there may arise during the performance year unexpected opportunities that must be seized at the moment with no need or time to write out objectives or perhaps even to know what to expect. Or it may not be possible or necessary to prescribe all results in advance for the work of a team member with an extra role such as a performance consultant.

The reason for question D1 is that two knowledgeable persons, one on the same team and someone outside the team need to be identified so that they can also answer questions C1-2 about the person's manner of performance. Appraisal of it is obviously more subjective and susceptible to self-serving bias than is appraisal of results. The two reviews, therefore, provide an independent perspective and thus add objectivity to that part of the appraisal. I believe this process is much better than the 360-degree group fudge.

Questions G1-2 are intended to flag appraisals for closer review in cases where there is an acknowledgment that data are insufficient and the appraisals may thus be more difficult to verify.

As long as they elicit the same kind of information, the appraisal questions actually used don't have to be identical to the ones I've suggested, but they do need to be the same for all individuals. If questions C1-2 about manner of performance seem too direct and possibly self-incriminating, less direct questions could be substituted, like these two:

C1. Feedback/rescue efforts from others about manner of performance?
C2. If yes, briefly describe what happened.

Step 3. Team members get two reviews of their manner of performance.

If the two reviewers identified in the "Me" appraisal concur with the person's answers to C1-2, they certify the answers. If one or both reviewers don't concur with the answers, they meet with the appraised person, ask for and review any documentation (e.g., of any formal monitoring or rescue efforts), and try to reach a consensus on the answers. If none is reached, that part of the appraisal is forwarded to the appraised person's team without certification, along with a documented basis for not having certified the answers.

**Step 4. Teams review/certify members' appraisals and self-appraise team
      performance.**

This step is in two stages, each carried out in a meeting.

Review/certify members' self-appraisals. In the first meeting, the review of performance on member's individual objectives ought to be fairly pro forma as long as objective and corroborating data are available. The same should be true in reviewing the answers to the questions on manner of performance if the answers had already been certified.

Where the team needs to concentrate its review obviously is on less substantiated appraisals, disputed appraisals, and any nominations for MVP. In arriving at decisions on these three types of cases when they occur, the team should get substantiating information if it's available or can be deduced (e.g., from team results). The team may also get more input from the two reviewers as well as from the appraised person in cases of uncertified appraisals of manner of performance. In cases where there is still uncertainty over what should be the final appraisal, the team may give the affected members the benefit of the doubt if reasonable to do so or may forward the appraisals onto the PRB for a final determination. However, these options shouldn't be taken until after the second meeting is held because it's possible its outcome could change any one or more of the members' self-appraisals.

The team will also need to respond constructively to any members who indicated in their answers to questions F1-2 that they want to develop horizontally through acquiring more performance skills. Various options are available if development would benefit the person and wouldn't disrupt the team's plans. A mentor or coach could be picked to help the person, roles could be exchanged within the team, an exchange with another team might be feasible, etc.

Self-appraise team performance. In the second meeting, the team appraises its own team performance. Someone outside the team who knows the team's performance relatively well (see question E1 in the "We" appraisal) should be invited to attend this second meeting to reinforce objectivity. The team does the "We" appraisal by answering questions like the ones I'm suggesting here:

The "We" Appraisal Questions

A1. How many team objectives?
A2. All met?
A3. Which one (s), if any, clearly exceeded, and what were the extra gains?
A4. Which objectives contributed directly to which company goals?
A5. Which ones, if any, were Alpine objectives?
A6. Any unexpected and very tough obstacles encountered?
A7. If yes, which objective (s) involved and, briefly, what happened?
B1. Anything (else) special about team's performance?
B2. If yes, briefly describe.
C1. Everyone's manner of performance consistently positive? (see Appendix C).
C2. If not, briefly describe what happened if not already documented.
D1. Which if any other teams contributed to your team's accomplishments and how so?
D2. To which if any teams' accomplishments did your team contribute and how so?
E1. Who else besides your team knows its performance relatively well?
E2. What other team (s)' performance does your team know relatively well?
F1. Nominate any team (s), including your own, for Most Valuable Team?
F2. If yes, who and briefly explain why.
G1. Data insufficient on results/any answers difficult to verify?
G2. If yes, identify and briefly explain why.

H1. Consensus reached by team on all answers?
H2. If not, identify disagreements and briefly explain why not.

You can see that most "We" questions are essentially comparable in content and purpose to the "Me" questions, including those intended to help the PRB determine whether some teams should receive a larger share of the company's performance bonus pool. Again, as long as they elicit the same kind of information, the appraisal questions actually used don't have to be identical to the ones I've suggested. But they do need to be the same for all teams.

Teams also don't have to follow the same procedure in answering the questions. For instance, team members could each answer the questions individually, share their answers, and then use some decision making process to reconcile any differences. Or members could answer the questions as a group and resolve any differences as they arise.

Step 5. The PRB resolves any disputed member appraisals and reviews/certifies all team appraisals.

Once the fourth step is done, teams send their self-appraisals of team performance, any unresolved appraisals of individual performance, and all accompanying documentation (e.g., data on results) to the PRB. It reviews the appraisals and all related documentation. It may ask a team to present its case or a team member to present his or her case and may also consult with any other knowledgeable teams or sources if there is reason to question an appraisal, such as in cases where there may be insufficient data or the team failed to reach consensus about its appraisal, or any nominations for MVT have been made. The PRB may change or leave unchanged any appraisal before certifying it. Any changes made in team appraisals may require revisiting member appraisals to see if any corresponding changes also need to be made in one or more of them.

Can Self-Appraisals Really be Honest?

There can never be guaranteed 100% honesty on performance appraisals. Yet I believe the procedure I've just described can certainly minimize dishonesty compared to what it has been throughout history. Moreover, I do think that most people most of the time in team settings can be trusted to give honest answers to self-appraisal questions when performance was short and the answers are consequential. I have several reasons for thinking so.

First, there is the nature of the appraisal itself. It's a series of mostly yes/no questions, not rating scales. It would take more than a fudge to answer "Yes" when the truth is "No." It would take a big, bald-faced lie because the difference between "Yes" and "No" is much more noticeable and verifiable than the subjective difference between two levels of a subjective rating scale. Making big, bald-faced lies requires more audacity and is thus less likely to be made, especially, too, when people know their appraisals will be reviewed for certification.

Second, trying to distort the truth through creative writing should be minimized because brevity, not embellishments, is requested in giving narrative answers.

Third, many of the questions ask for readily verifiable answers. For instance, whether an objective has been met can be verified by comparing the documented results obtained to the criteria (e.g., timeliness) that were stated in the written objective. And on the more sensitive and less objective questions relating to manner of performance, there should be an evidentiary trail from any formal monitoring required and from any further interventions (e.g., through the use of PIPs) in cases where that part of performance hadn't been consistently positive.

Fourth, a person's performance in the "glass-house" of a team-based organization is often on view or known about, whether by members of real or virtual teams. It would likely take a conspiracy of two or more people to conceal a falsehood (granted, it's certainly not impossible for that to happen).

Fifth, honesty isn't left up to unguarded trust. There are several means of guarded trust built into the procedure, such as having two reviewers for the self-appraisal of manner of performance.

Sixth, and finally, falsehoods when uncovered face possible punishment. Falsifying an appraisal is an unethical act and should not be tolerated.

Other Considerations

Neither a book like this nor any appraisal guidelines can or should be definitive. Situations will invariably arise that will need to be considered in doing the appraisals. I'll discuss two situations. One is when people move among different teams. If a person changes to another team during the performance year, for example, the appraisal at the end of the performance year should cover manner of performance while on both teams and only on those objectives for which there was sufficient time to complete them. If one or more objectives have to be cancelled, the appraisal should cover performance on them only if the cancellation was caused by poor performance.

The other situation has to do with the life span of appraisals. Obviously, individuals may keep copies of their certified appraisals for as long as they wish. But for how long should appraisals be kept by the organization? One way to make paper work rather than make paperwork is to be sensible about record keeping. I see no practical reason to keep more than the last three appraisals. If a negative appraisal is made, it should be expunged when and if there are two subsequent and consecutive positive appraisals certified.

There are many other nuances that could be considered. Indeed, in the past I've written reams of policies for bureaucracies so that many other nuances could be covered. I want to spare you that ordeal. Empowered people ought to be able to wing it the rest of the way.

Let's go now to the next and final chapter so you can see my suggestions for linking sanctions to the "We" and "Me" appraisals.

Chapter 8. Sanctioning Performance

WHAT THE PRINCIPLES ADVISE DOING

- Responsibly empower the sanctioning.
- Sanction positive success differently from negative success.
- Sanction positive failure differently from negative failure.
- Link, not lock, sanctions to performance.

REWARDING TALL PERFORMANCE

Books have been written just on the subject of rewards. There are so many different kinds of rewards, and it's possible to get very detailed about each. All I want to do in this chapter is sketch how one kind of reward, performance bonuses (lump-sum cash awards) can be done consistent with the principles and within the We/Me framework. Every organization should consider offering bonuses (they are usually part of a larger incentive package that may include profit sharing, stock options, or other forms of rewards). If bonuses aren't given for tall performance, then some other form of reward certainly should be given.

Before going to the We/Me model for awarding bonuses, these eight points that are either part of or in addition to the principles need to be heeded when designing a bonus system or any other monetary reward system:

- Make rewards valued and targeted.
- Customize rewards.
- Reward positive failures when justified.
- Don't tolerate negative successes.
- Think twice before rewarding ethical behavior itself.
- Don't reward with merit pay.
- Reward both teams and individuals for tall performance.
- Be open about rewards.

To motivate performance, rewards must be valued. If not, the organization has wasted its money, and there's no room for waste in a highly competitive marketplace. For a reward to be valued, it must be seen as worth the effort to get, and the effort must be seen as linked to the reward. In other words, the individual or team must want the reward and also see that getting it will depend on their tall performance. Rewards of trivial value or ones handed out capriciously will be counterproductive. It's not enough for a reward to be valued, however. Even when it is, the company will have wasted its money and perhaps worse (lose customers, e.g.,) if the reward wasn't targeted for the meeting of performance expectations in line with the company's business strategy and goals. Examples abound where companies rewarded one set of behaviors (handling many customers, e.g.) when instead they should have rewarded a different set (handling customers well, e.g.).

People value rewards differently. Some people, for example, may value bonuses far less than one or more of the other parts of the total compensation package. The implication for the organization of these individual differences in preferences is that recruitment either needs to be targeted toward people whose compensation preferences are similar or that the compensation package needs to be individually tailored, including whether to include bonuses. Where there's empowerment, customization probably is inevitable.

The organization may decide to offer some form of monetary reward of lesser value for positive failures, particularly when extraordinary effort and ingenuity was put forward to no avail (recall the story of the risk takers). In any case, the organization needs to resolve never to penalize positive failures.

Rewarding, or even tolerating, negative success is doubly unethical when the success was achieved unethically and knowingly so. The act of rewarding or tolerating an unethical act becomes an unethical act itself, and one that begets more unethical acts. Success achieved unethically, therefore, must be penalized if the value of ethical behavior is to be preserved. Negative successes achieved despite other short behaviors, such as inefficient ones, need not necessarily be penalized, but no organization can afford for long to tolerate them.

It is debatable whether ethical behavior itself should be rewarded. An argument against doing so is that behaving ethically is an obligation of everyone and should not be considered an extra effort to be singled out for a reward. The opposing argument is that being ethical indeed requires extra effort, and anyone who makes it should be rewarded. I waver between the two arguments (and in any case, empowered people should decide what to do about it). What I am certain about, though, is that ethical behavior must never be penalized.

Merit pay is a salary increment based on performance and should never, never in my opinion, be used in any organization, short or tall (but I never could persuade the US government to stop wasting taxpayers' money in giving merit pay to its civil servants). Merit pay is conceptually mistaken. Salary is the basic pay part of a total compensation program, not a reward for performance during a particular performance year. Merit pay is also the most cost ineffective of all possible monetary rewards. They are rarely if ever withdrawn when there is a performance decrement at the end of the next year. So the salary increment lives on to death as an annuity. Moreover, when the conventional performance appraisal rating is fudged upwards by a supervisor to favor a subordinate (as often happens), merit pay is tantamount to being a gift that keeps on giving.

Both individual team members and the team itself need to be eligible for monetary rewards (unless the team decides otherwise). There is always the possibility that the tallest performance of one member is what makes the team excel, and everyone on the team knows it. As I've already said, not to reward this MVP is to risk alienating or losing him or her, but giving the MVP substantially more money or not rewarding the (positively) successful team at all risks sowing dissension among the rest of its members.

Coming now to the last point, hierarchies are usually very secretive about who gets how much pay and rewards. Holding power depends partly on withholding knowledge from others. Besides being a handmaiden to power, secrecy also has several other faults. It breeds mistrust. It fuels discontent when peers overestimate the money each person is making. And it diminishes the motivational potential of rewards in that people need to see whenever tall performance of anyone in the organization gets rewarded and whether it seems warranted.

Abiding by the principles and the points just made, I have put three steps into the We/Me model for linking performance bonuses to performance appraisals.

1. Guidelines are created.
2. The PRB awards the "We" bonus shares to deserving teams.
3. Teams award the "Me" bonus shares to their deserving members.

People are empowered to adopt or adapt these steps to suit themselves while keeping the principles and points in mind.

Step 1. Guidelines are created.

Let's suppose that guidelines have been crafted by either the Steering Council or the PRB that reflect these decisions:

- Bonuses may not be available if the company's annual goals aren't met.
- All teams and individuals may be eligible for bonuses.
- "We" will be put before "Me" in bonus considerations.
- Any negative successes will be set aside for subsequent consideration.
- Consensus will be sought in decisions about bonuses.
- All decisions will be documented and openly available.
- Due process will be made available for proposed penalties.
- The PRB will allocate bonus shares to the teams.
- The teams will allocate their bonus shares internally.
- Any MVPs and MVTs will be eligible for meaningfully larger bonuses.
- Only positive successes and positive failures will be eligible for bonuses.
- Anyone may exchange bonus eligibility for equivalent compensation.
- Neither trivial nor extravagant bonuses will be awarded.
- Ethical behavior may be rewarded but only if exemplary.

Step 2. The PRB awards the "We" bonus shares to deserving teams.

Once all appraisals are certified, the PRB decides whether none, some, or all teams deserve bonus shares and whether any differences in performance justify larger shares. The PRB comes to this decision after putting the appraisals of team performance into qualitatively different categories.

The first two categories would be for teams in which all members' manner of performance was consistently positive and all objectives were met. But the first category would be reserved for any teams with patterns of appraisal answers (to the questions I cited in the previous chapter for differentiating among tall performances) that demonstrated even taller performance. Any teams in this first category would get larger shares. Most of the teams would presumably be in the second category and would get smaller shares.

A third category would be for any cases of positive failure where all members' manner of performance was consistently positive, but one or more objectives weren't met. Whether any still smaller shares are awarded to teams in this category would depend on the specifics of each particular case and on whether the remainder of the bonus fund would allow meaningful shares.

A fourth and final category would be for any cases of negative success or negative failure. No team in this last category should be considered for a bonus share unless the shortfalls in behavior were those of one or more team members having had absolutely no role in the objective (s) involved. I recommend such an exception because it's possible to have short performance from one or more team members and still meet and even exceed the team objectives in question.

Step 3. Teams award the "Me" bonus shares to their deserving members.

Once a team has received its bonus share, monies from it can be allocated among the members according to whatever rationale the team chooses consistent with the guidelines. For example, the team could emulate the PRB's procedure and put its members' certified appraisals into comparable categories and then decide on bonus allocations among and within the eligible categories. The team could also decide to set aside some of the money for use by the whole team.

PENALIZING CERTAIN SHORT PERFORMANCES

It's perhaps fitting to wait, or to procrastinate, until now to deal with the last aspect of accountability and follow-up, that of punishment. Procrastination isn't what is needed, of course, but it seems to be a natural response, and that's perfectly understandable. Punishment is an unpleasant subject, task, and experience, even if it's euphemized and practiced sometimes as "positive discipline." Yet punishment is meant to be an unpleasant experience. Otherwise, the prospect of it wouldn't be a potential deterrent. Moreover, without justified punishment, there would be no accountability. So we must deal with punishment and deal with it in the most efficacious and ethical way possible.

Penalties are as assorted as rewards are and range from informal, mild rebukes to formal responses like dismissal and even beyond (e.g., criminal prosecution for serious wrongdoing). Penalties have also generated their own share of study and controversy. Two arguments against their use are that they do not work and are unethical. I disagree with both arguments. If done properly, punishment does work and is ethical. To be done properly, these seven points need to be heeded:

- Penalize the won't do's and wrong do's, not the can't do's.
- Don't penalize without providing the option of due process.
- Fit the penalty to the offense.
- Penalize sooner than later.
- Penalize publicly

- Avoid upside-down incentives.
- Penalize individuals, not teams.

Punishment is for the won't do and wrong do behaviors. Punishment obviously shouldn't be the response to can't do behaviors. New knowledge and/or skill are the answer there. But if that doesn't work, dismissal may be the answer, and dismissal in such instances is not punishment but rather a necessary remedy for an intractable problem (dismissal can be done constructively by, for example, trying to help the person find another job-but not by withholding truthful information from prospective employers who inquire about the person).

The won't do's and the wrong do's and the doer responsible for them must be verified before meting out a penalty. Punishing mistakenly obviously is an injustice. A due process to allow for verification or exoneration needs to be inserted between the incident and the punishment.

Punishment must fit the offense, neither too lenient nor too draconian. Much punishment is a misfit, generally being seen as too lenient. Because the aftermath of lenient penalties can be worse than that of lenient rewards (a lenient penalty, for example, is likely to be followed by more offenses), the link between penalties and performance should be tighter than between rewards and performance. On the other hand, the link should not be so tight as to turn it into a lock, since each case needs to be considered in terms of its own circumstances.

Punishment must be timely. Inertia or procrastination delays punishment. Waiting until after the year-end appraisal to account for punishable behaviors occurring much earlier obviously is an avoidable delay. An unduly long due process also delays punishment (in some bureaucracies, due process seems to be an enterprise all to itself, tying up many people who could be really working instead). Delays create problems by allowing time for more of the same short behaviors or worse (snowballing downhill) and causing disrespect for workplace justice.

Punishment must be publicized, but responsibly so. The adage, "for justice to be done, it must be seen as done," has double meaning. People who know about the offensive behavior but do not know about the unpublished punishment will tend to think the punishment did not happen or was too lenient. And the knowledge that punishment will be published is itself intended to be a deterrent to others.

Worth repeating, ethical behavior in particular and positive failure in general must never be punished. Every time they are, which is often, wrongdoing is given a badvantage. A prime example of upside-down, badvantageous punishment is the retaliation by an organization against a member who has blown the whistle validly on wrongdoing by other members of the organization.

Penalties aren't analogous to rewards. Penalties are for short behaviors. Rewards are for tall behaviors and tall results. Since a team can't behave, per se, penalties shouldn't be applied to it for punishable behaviors by one or more of its members.

Given these conditions and principles, I recommend something like the following four steps in the We/Me model for penalizing the won't do's and wrong do's:

1. Guidelines are created.
2. The PRB develops a general guide on punishable behaviors.
3. Teams, with exceptions, apply guide as needed.
4. A due process is developed and made available.

Step 1. Guidelines are created.

Let's suppose either the Steering Council or the PRB has crafted these guidelines:

- A general guide on penalties will be developed and followed.
- Penalties will be chosen and applied, usually by the teams.
- Any team may surrender some or all responsibility to the PRB.
- A due process is developed and made available.
- Record keeping will be the same as for appraisals.

Step 2. The PRB develops a general guide on punishable behaviors

While penalties should be decided on a case-by-case basis in order to consider any unique circumstances, some uniformity and consistency are needed across cases to minimize arbitrariness. A company-wide, general guide can help provide that structured flexibility in contrast to a table of penalties that tightly locks them to specific offenses. I have suggested in Appendix C how such a guide could be developed.

Step 3. Teams, with exceptions, apply guide as needed.

Punishing its own members is probably the most difficult task a team ever has to face. If that's so, why have them face it? The answer is threefold. First, a team is fully empowered without limits. It shouldn't shirk any of its responsibilities, no matter how unpleasant. Second, the team is in the best position to penalize its wayward members (in the true spirit of empowerment, a person could be allowed to suggest his or her own penalty). They know each other's performance, tall and short, better than anybody else. And by solving their problems of short performance, I believe they strengthen, not weaken, themselves through the experience. Third, while difficult, the task isn't an impossible one. Teams have the guide to follow and they can seek advice from the PRB.

Nevertheless, because punishment can be an onerous task, any team should, if it chooses, be allowed to surrender some or all of its punishment responsibilities. But any team that does so should risk losing certain eligibilities, such as, for instance, bonuses or the maximum on any pay-for-skills salary plan since the team is forfeiting one of its the roles.

Step 4. A due process is developed and made available.

It's always possible that the wrong person might be punished or might be punished too harshly given mitigating circumstances. Therefore, anyone facing the prospect of punishment should have the right to nullify or reduce the impending punishment by making an appeal to an independent hearing board and to have the appeal heard by that board.

Due process is quasi judicial and requires a careful balancing of structure and flexibility for the sake of fairness and justice. To keep flexibility within reasonable bounds here, all teams should follow the same due process. Therefore, it needs to be designed by either the PRB or the Steering Council and then followed by everyone. But the process needs to be as streamlined as possible so that justice is both swift and sure. All absolutely unnecessary requirements need to be avoided, such as purely bureaucratic procedures that have little or no value. Additionally, due process should be reserved for only the more serious offenses and harsher penalties.

Any person for whom punishment is being considered needs, of course, to know about that consideration and the right to appeal it. If appealed, punishment obviously must be delayed or there can be no due process.

The appellant should be encouraged to marshal all relevant documentation in support of the appeal. The appellant should also be encouraged to invite one or a few more supporters to testify at the hearing. One or more of the appellant's team in favor of the proposed punishment should be required to testify at the hearing, as should be any dissenting member (s).

The conduct of hearings should be formal and follow a protocol. The team's representative (s) proposing the punishment should testify first, followed by the appellant and any supporters. At the end of the hearing, the appeal board should recess, reach a decision in seclusion, and then return to announce it. The board's decision should be final.

The process, its resulting decisions, and their effects need to be carefully monitored to avoid any deviations if the process is working well or to change the process if it isn't working well.

We have now come to the end of how the model could be used for punishment, but not without first ending on a more upbeat note. If the right people are hired into the organization and performance is managed well from beginning to end, then punishment hopefully won't have to be used.

Gary B. Brumback

Notes and References for the Text

Introduction to Part One

1. Semler R. (1989). Managing without managers. *Harvard Business Review*, <u>67</u>, 76-84.
2. Ciulla, JB. (2000). *The working life: The promise and betrayal of modern work.* New York, NY: Times Books.

Chapter 1.

1. Foster, RR. & Kaplan, S. (2000). *Creative destruction: Why companies that are built to last under perform the market-and how to successfully transform them.* New York, NY: Currency.
2. The late W. Edwards Deming, for example, who was one of the "fathers" of the TQM movement, believed that systems alone determined how well individuals would perform.
3. I'm indebted to Thomas S. McFee, former Assistant Secretary of Personnel Administration for the US Department of Health and Human Services, for suggesting to me the term "manner of performance" as a synonym for behaviors.
4. Associated Press. (1997, August 24). Class gives execs lessons in etiquette. *The News-Journal.*
5. Murphy, E. (2002). The best corporate citizens perform better financially. *Business Ethics*, March-April, 13.
6. Josephson, M. (1988). Teaching ethical decision-making and principled reasoning. *Ethics: Easier Said than Done*, <u>1</u>, 27-33.
7. Torry, S. (1994, September 5). Harassment case award strikes a chord with firms. *The Washington Post.*
8. Estes, R. *(1996). Tyranny of the bottom line: Why corporations make good people do bad things.* San Francisco: Berrett-Koehler Publishers.
9. Estes, <u>op cit.</u>
10. Punch, M. (1996). *Dirty business: Exploring corporate misconduct. Analyses and cases.* London: Sage Publications.
11. Cameron, KS. et al. (1991). Best practices in white-collar downsizing: Managing contradictions. *Academy of Management Executive*, <u>5</u>, 57-73.
12. Kidwell, RE. (1995). Pink slips without tears. *Academy of Management Executive.* <u>9</u>, 69-70.
13. Pfeffer, J. (1998). *The human equation: Building profits by putting people first.* Cambridge, MA: Harvard Business School Press.

Chapter 2

1. Josephson, M. (1989). Holding the top man accountable. *Ethics: Easier Said Than Done*, 1989, 2, 26.
2. O'Toole, J. (1995). *Vanguard management: Redesigning the corporate future*. Garden City, NJ: Doubleday.

Chapter 3.

1. Specter, M. (2001). Rethinking the brain: How the songs of canaries upset a fundamental principle of science. *The New Yorker*, 42-53.
2. Ryff, CD. (1995). Psychological well being in adult life. *Current Directions in Psychological Science*. 4, 99-104.
3. Maslow, A. (1954). *Motivation and Personality*, New York: Harper.
4. Byham, WC. & Cox J. (1988). *Zapp! The lightning of empowerment*. New York: Fawcett Columbine.
5. Kester, JD. (2001). Bandura: Beliefs, bobo, and behavior. *APS Observer*, 14, 8-9.
6. Carr, C. (1992). *Teampower: Lessons from America's top companies on putting teampower to work*. Englewood Cliffs, NJ: Prentice-Hall.
7. Semler, R. (1989). Managing without managers. *Harvard Business Review*, 67, 76-84, 78.
8. Robinson E. (1993, December 8). Toni Morrison's measured words. *The Washington Post*.
9. Ackroyd, S. & Thompson, P. (1999). *Organizational Misbehavior*, London: Sage.
10. Lawler, E.E. III. (2000). *Rewarding excellence: Pay strategies for the new economy*. San Francisco: Jossey-Bass.
11. Manz, CC. & Sims, HP Jr. (1993). *Business without bosses: How self-managing teams are building high-performing companies*. New York, NY: John Wiley & Sons, Inc.
12. Cloke, K. & Goldsmith, J. (2002). *The end of management and the rise of organizational democracy*. San Francisco: Jossey-Bass.
13. Koch, R. & Godden, I. (1996). *Managing without management: A post-management manifesto for business simplicity*. London: Nicholas Brealey Publishing.
14. Perl, P. (1984, September 3). High-tech methods boost productivity, but at a cost. *The Washington Post*, A28.
15. Hawkins, D. (1997, September 15). Who's watching now? *US News and World Report*, 56-57.
16. Peters, TJ. & Waterman, RH. Jr. (1982). *In search of excellence*. New York: Warner Books.
17. Taylor, FT. (1911). *Scientific Management*, New York: Harper & Brothers.
18. Byrne, JA. (1993, December 20). The horizontal corporation, *Business Week*, 76-81.

19. Wellins, RS., Byham, WC., & Dixon, GR. (1994). *Inside teams: How 20 world-class organizations are winning through teamwork.* San Francisco: Jossey-Bass, 339.
20. Byrne, JA. (August 30, 1999). The global corporation becomes the leaderless corporation. *Business Week,* **88-89.**
21. Semler, *op cit.* 20.
22. Manz, CC. & Simms, HP. Jr., (2001). *The new superleadership:Leading others to lead themselves.* San Francisco: Berrett-Koehler.
23. Wellins, RS., Byham WC., & Wilson, JM. (1991). *Empowered teams: Creating self-directed work groups that improve quality, productivity, and participation.* San Francisco: Jossey-Bass.

Chapter 4.

1. Katzenbach, JR. (2000). Peak performance: Aligning the hearts and minds of your employees. Boston: Harvard Business School Press.
2. Eden, D. (1988). Pygmalion, goal setting, and expectancy: Compatible ways to boost productivity. *Academy of Management Review,* 13, 639-652.
3. Weick, KE. (1982). Misconceptions about managerial productivity. Paper presented at the Cornell-in-New York Lecture Series, Cornell Club, New York City.

Introduction to Part Two

1. Gabor, A. (June 5, 1989). Catch a falling star system: Firms see ways to make team players of their lone rangers. *U.S. News & World Report,* 43-44.
2. Biech, E. (2001). The Pfeiffer book of successful team-building tools. San Francisco, CA: Jossey-Bass.
3. Harper, B. & Harper, A. (1992). *Succeeding as a self-directed work team: 20 important questions answered.* Mohegan Lake, NY: MW Corporation.
4. Orsburn, JD. et al. (1990). *Self-directed work teams: The new American challenge.* Homewood, IL: Business One Irwin.
5. Ray, D. & Bronstein, H. (1995). *Teaming up: Making the transition to a self-directed team-based organization.* New Yprk, NY: McGraw-Hill, Inc.
6. Brumback, GB. (1996). Getting the right people ethically. *Public Personnel Management,* 25, 267-276.
7. Purser, RE. & Cabana, S. (1998). *The self-managing organization: How leading companies are transforming the work of teams for real impact* New York, NY: The Free Press.

Chapter 5.

1. Mathews, MC. (1988). *Strategic interventions in organizations: Resolving ethical dilemmas*. New Bury Park: Sage
2. Thompson, KR., Hochwarter, WA., & Mathys, NJ. (1997). Stretch targets: What makes them effective? *Academy of Management Executive*, <u>11</u>, 48-59, p. 48.
3. McNamee, T. & Land, G. (1994). Backwards from perfect: A process for involving the customer. In Conference Proceedings. *Creating a customer-driven government*. Washington, DC: Federal Quality Institute, 597-607.

Chapter 6.

1. Ivancevich, JM. & McMahon, JT. (1982). The effects of goal setting, external feedback, and self-generated feedback on outcome variables: A field experiment. *Academy of Management Journal*, <u>25</u>, 359-372.
2. Meyer, C. (1994). How the right measures help teams excel. *Harvard Business Review*, <u>72</u>, 95-103.

Chapter 7.

1. Brumback, GB. (1991). The unemployment-at-will doctrine. *Labor Law Journal*, <u>45</u>, 111-115.
2. Weaver, GR. <u>et al.</u> (1999). Integrated and decoupled corporate social performance: Management commitments, external pressures, and corporate ethics practices. *The Academy of Management Journal*, <u>42</u>, 539-552.
3. Vandaveer, VV. (1998). As we enter the twenty-first century. *The Industrial Psychologist*, <u>35</u>, 99-102.

Appendices

I felt the book would flow more smoothly if I put certain material into appendices. I think you'll find them relevant and useful.

Appendix A. Envisioning and Valuing a Culture of Tall Performance

Appendix B. Tall Objectives Closer Up

Appendix C. How to Create and Use Examples of Short Behaviors

Appendix D. A Resource Guide for Rescuing Falling Performance

Appendix E. Good Decisions and Good Conflict

Appendix F. The History of MBR

Appendix A. Valuing And Envisioning A Culture Of Tall Performance

An organization's culture comprises its values and visions and, most importantly, the actions associated with them. In a review of the literature, a business professor concluded that the right organizational culture leads to "sustained superior financial performance."[1] The We/Me model is an ideal way to mainstream and reinforce the company's vision and values that have already been put in place before the MBR process begins. That's why I put them in place in setting the stage for Part Two. In this appendix I discuss their importance and suggest how they might be put into place in a real company.

Personal and Organizational Values

Our personal values denote anything that we value either as ends in them selves or means to ends. What we value can include ideas, experiences, objects, people, and practically anything else imaginable, but with a caveat. Valuing people primarily or solely as a means is an exploitative and is thus an unethical stance toward those people. To be sure, people are a means to tall performance, but the "human" in "human resources" needs to be underscored. As "Alice," the character in the popular Dilbert comic strip once put it as she screamed at "Catbert, Evil HR Director," "We're people, not resources!"[2]

The late psychologist, Milton Rokeach, spent much of his career studying personal values, and I like what he found and did. He developed a way to measure what he had discovered through research to be 18 "instrumental values," or valued means, and 18 "terminal values," or valued ends.[3] A person, for example, who wants to make a lasting contribution in his/her life's endeavors and chooses to do so honestly, ambitiously, and responsibly is a person who values a "sense of accomplishment" as an end and values "honesty, ambition, and responsibility" as the means to that end. The only adjustments I would make to his work would be to add tall performance as a terminal value and to make explicit among the instrumental values the 10 ethical values I mentioned in the first chapter. Upholding these 10 values is an imperative for positive success in business.

People tend not to think about their values unless they are challenged or substantive decisions have to be made. But a person's values can be inferred from the person's behavior, including decision- making. That's precisely why our values are so important. They strongly influence what we do and will not do and how we construe and sometimes misconstrue what is going on around us and in the world. Consider, for example, myself as a law abiding, tax paying citizen. While I file honest tax records partly because I fear getting caught and punished if I don't, mostly I abide by the tax laws because I think it's the responsible and honest thing to do. I value responsibility and honesty. I chose this very personal example because filing these records and paying taxes challenges my values when I think of the vast amount of taxes collected by various levels of government and how they are spent and misspent.

Organizations can be said to have values, too, in the sense that desired means and ends are explicitly enunciated, desired, shared, promoted, and practiced by their people. "Practice" is the operative word. Preaching values and not practicing them is both hypocritical and foolish, and can come back to haunt the preacher. I'm reminded of the corporation that got haunted by a strike, bad publicity, and soured customer relations partly because it's preached value of "imagination" was contradicted by a policy requiring operatives to follow a script in telephone exchanges with customers.[4]

Living up to good values in the conduct of business, on the other hand, can enhance business performance. This rather obvious conclusion is supported not only by common sense but also by research, consulting, and actual business experience. For instance, researchers at Indiana University concluded from their review of other studies and also from the findings of their own research that "strongly held, shared values" lead to superior organizational performance.[5] A similar conclusion that organizational excellence is most associated with "clear, consistent, and serious values" comes from a consultant who has worked with "scores" of client organizations.[6] The value of practicing good values is not lost on some business people, either. Here, for instance, is what the chairman/CEO of a well-known and very successful (in a very positive way) dry-goods corporation had to say on the matter: "A company's values-what it stands for, what its people believe in-are crucial to its competitive success. Indeed, values drive the business."[7]

The only way values can drive an organization, of course, is by driving its members. A financial goal, for example, will not be a driving force as an ends value unless the members feel their personal financial security is at risk and/or they have a strong sense of commitment and make a personal contribution to that goal. Moreover, and perhaps not surprisingly, financial goals are not even the most driving values among some of the more financially successful companies.[8] The most powerful values an organization can have are usually the qualitative, softer, and less concrete ones that reflect members' needs to develop and use their talents and to be empowered to use them. One of the values at the dry-goods maker, for example, is empowerment, and at "Three Circles," empowerment is practiced in the name of three values, democracy, profit sharing, and sharing and using information.

Some other qualitative values explicitly enunciated by organizations that also have the potential to inspire and motivate their members include the following that I have selected from my own file of samples of business value statements: "Share our strengths, strengthen our teams." "Have fun" (that one sounds like a great place to work for anyone who has a wholesome, balanced perspective on work). "Be the best." "Be innovative." "Accept risks" (I would clarify that to read "accept risks of positive failure"). "Be imaginative."

Psychologist Michael Maccoby, author of *Why Work*, even believes such softer values are biologically necessary for motivating and guiding behavior.[9] In other words, we don't and can't live by bread alone.

Values are particularly helpful in guiding organizations during times of change, which nowadays is often. When it comes time to pick a new leader for a business, for instance, the successor needs to be someone who isn't at odds with the company's values. Of course, strongly held values that are out of step with inevitable change could cause the organization to stay out of step. A highly valued technology invented years ago within a company, for example, may be held onto far too long.

Ethical values, however, are never wrong or out of step at anytime, and adhering to them in our actions is absolutely necessary for performing tall. They thus need to be the bedrock for all of the other positive values people and their organizations hold. The function of the ethical values is not so much to energize us, but to help channel like a river our energy toward right doing and away from wrongdoing. But the bedrock must not be out of sight and out of mind like a code of ethics typically is nor only implied in any of the organization's other pronouncements about its values. Ethics is both too frail a human condition and too important to be "muted."[10] The principled actions in Part Two go well beyond muteness to mainstream the ethical values into the MBR process without being "moralistic" about it.

I put quotes around "moralistic" because this may be as good a place as any to make sure my view of ethics vis-à-vis morality and religious beliefs isn't misunderstood. What triggers my wanting to do this here is my remembering a gentleman in the audience who came up to me after a talk I had given on quality, ethics, and accountability.[11] During the talk I had been using the terms "ethical values" and "moral values" interchangeably. He suggested that I only use the adjective, "ethical," in referring to the universal values. To him, morality connoted religious beliefs and had no place in business and government. While I certainly didn't invoke any religious beliefs in my talk, I decided from then on to follow his advice to avoid any future misunderstandings. I also agree with him that religion and secular endeavors don't mix well. America's founders felt the same way.

Personal and Organizational Visions

A personal vision of one self is what a person wants to become or attain in the future, and an organizational vision is what its people want the organization to become or attain in the future. If they are to be players instead of spectators at their future's unfolding, therefore, people and organizations need to have viable visions of that future for themselves and to go after those visions with vim and vigor.

I can think of four prerequisites to having a viable organizational vision. One is to have a realistic but flexible and open-minded self-image or identity. Think of the buggy whip makers before the advent of the "horseless carriage." They had a realistic image of themselves as skilled craftsmen, but they rigidly stuck to making their whips better and better.[12] Of course, any company that ventures too far away from the business it's in is asking for trouble. A business consultant and book author on the subject argues that in the course of doing business a company must remain loyal to its identity or risk going out of business.[13] But I would argue that unless there's some flexibility and open-mindedness about the identity, the fate of the whip makers may await the business. Now consider an example of another identity, namely, that of "being a world-class bottle maker." It could, with a little flexibility and open-mindedness, very well be stretched to entertain the possibility of becoming a "world-class container maker."

A second prerequisite is to have a futuristic orientation. It's deceptively simple, but in reality we may feel hobbled by the past on our back, we may only see the present, and we may only worry about the future (worrying about the future is a can't-do orientation). Even where you would expect to find them in abundance, that is, coming from people near and at the top of their hierarchies, futuristic orientations don't surface readily as can-do and will-do behaviors. In one of the hottest articles ever to appear in the *Harvard Business* Review, the authors argued that American business is mismanaging itself through its myopia.[14] I have put into Appendix C examples of short-nosed behaviors that don't make for tall performance in the future.

A third prerequisite is to have a solid commitment to the vision, which, when coupled with some sign of progress toward the vision could go a long way toward holding short-term pressures at bay. But getting a commitment from people in a command and control organization on a vision (or anything else) may very well be futile. The prospects for widespread commitment are infinitely much brighter in a lowerarchy, especially if members participate in doing the envisioning. Indeed, it makes good sense in such an organization for its leader to seek involvement by everyone in shaping a vision of the organization rather than seeking their commitment to his or her own vision. As the president of Three Circles discovered, and not to his dismay, everyone else in the organization may be more right than the leader.

The fourth prerequisite is to have a strategic plan. If there is no strategy on how to reach the vision, then it most likely won't be reached. Unfortunately strategic planning is so difficult to do well that sometimes people who most certainly should do it just don't do it.[15] The founder of one company defiantly proclaimed that he and his people are doers, not planners.[16] The two basic tenets of their "Theory Q" outlook are "be informed" and "don't bother to plan." I sympathize with their theory, but I must disagree with it. Being informed already gives one a leg up on planning. And other than dumb luck, I simply don't know of any other way to realizing an organizational vision than through strategically planning for it and then following through on it. Doing strategic planning well, however, should not be confused with doing it better. Better is the enemy of good enough when it comes to planning. As I've said, plan for change, and be prepared to change your plan.

THE FUTURE SEARCH CONFERENCE

Several companies have successfully used the future search conference as an empowering way to envision a new future, create a new culture to support the vision, and to develop a strategy for getting there.[17] The basic premise of the conference is two-fold. First, either shape the future or be at its mercy. Second, people throughout the organization should do the shaping since every member has a stake in the matter and something to contribute in the shaping. What follows next is my overview of how I think a search conference should proceed.

If the organization is a large hierarchy, a cross section of all members is invited to attend. Although focused on the future, the agenda begins with a brief review of the organization's past so that everyone has a common understanding of the firm's origin, its traditions (some of which may be worth keeping), and how and why it evolved into the hierarchy it is. This historical review also provides a starting point for discerning any trends that have had an impact on the organization.

Next, the present status of every key feature of the organization is reviewed along with a determination of why the overall performance of the business is stagnant or sagging (if it weren't one or the other, the organization's leadership might not have entertained radical changes in the first place). The review should include a look at the organization's present vision and prevailing values as well as its ethical climate. Prevailing values can be inferred from the organization's important decisions and practices and/or through a ready-made survey (e.g., of Rokeach's means and ends values). The organization's ethical climate can also be assessed through a ready-made survey, but any one selected needs to be supplemented with questions about the existence of badvantages.

The crux of the conference is the final stage in which conferees search for and settle on a future image of the organization, that, if realized, would not only be very different from but also much better than the present state of affairs. This time, for each key feature of the organization, conferees should answer a question like this: "What do we want this feature to be like five years from now?" Consider, for instance, the organization's current vision. If it doesn't convey the image of tall performance, the conferees should decide if that's an image that would inspire them and thus one to which they could become committed. Or consider the company's core business. People in one company were so ashamed of their main product that they replaced it with a different and more socially acceptable one that could be made using the same technology. Obviously, the shameful product wasn't consonant with the idea of tall performance.

Before answering the question about preferred values, the ethical values, and other "soft" values such as that of tall performance should be discussed. Before answering the question about a preferred organizational structure, the six imperatives for empowerment should be debated. Before answering the question about a preferred way to manage performance, an overview of the We/Me model and its underlying principles should be presented and discussed, naturally.

Once a future for each feature has been settled upon, a short and simple vision held by the conferees that captures the essence of the desired future needs to be written.

Before the conference concludes, task forces need to be created to work on action plans for making the desired changes in the features. Taken together, these plans become the organization's strategy for controlling its future rather than being controlled by it.

NOTES AND REFERENCES FOR APPENDIX A

1. Barney, JB. (1986). Organizational culture: Can it be a source of sustained competitive advantage? *Academy of Management Review*, <u>11</u>, 656-665.
2. Adams, S. (1996). *The Dilbert principle: A cubicle's-eye view of bosses, meetings, management fads & other workplace afflictions*. New York: Harper Business. I'd never heard of Dilbert until my book review editor

gave me this book to review. I am glad he did. My review was published in *Personnel Psychology*, 1997, <u>50</u>, 514-517.

3. Rokeach, M. (1973). *The nature of human values*. New York: Free Press.
4. Seglin, JL. (2000, September 9). The values statement vs. corporate reality. *The New York Times*.
5. Enz, CA. & Schwenk, C. (1989, August). Performance and the sharing of organizational values. Paper presented at the annual meeting of the Academy of Management.
6. Weiss, A. (1989). The value system. *Personnel Administrator*, <u>34</u>, 240-241.
7. Howard, R. (1990). Values make the company: An interview with Robert Haas. *Harvard Business Review*, <u>68</u>, 133-144.
8. Peters, TJ. & Waterman, RH Jr. (1982). *In search of excellence*. New York: Warner Books.
9. Maccoby, M. (1988). *Why work: Leading the new generation*. New York: Simon & Schuster.
10. Bird, FB. & Waters, JA. (1989). The moral muteness of managers. *California Management Review*, <u>32</u>, 73-88.
11. Brumback, GB. (1994). Total accountability, ethics, and quality. In T. Clements (Ed.). *Creating a customer-driven government*. Washington, DC: Federal Quality Institute.
12. McGowan, WG. (1986). What business are we really in? The question revisited. *Sloan Management Review*, <u>28</u>, 59-62.
13. Ackerman, LD. (2000). *Identity is destiny: Leadership and the roots of value creation*. San Francisco: Barrett-Koehler.
14. Hayes, RH. & Abernathy, WJ. (1980). Managing our way to economic decline. *Harvard Business Review*, <u>58</u>, 67-77.
15. Brumback, GB. (1980). Human planning: Failures, causes, needed research and education. *Academic Psychology Bulletin*, <u>2</u>, 179-186.
16. Kehrer, DM. (1989, Sept.). The miracle of theory Q. *Business Month*, 45-49.
17. Purser, RE. & Cabana, S. (1998). *The self-managing organization: How leading companies are transforming the work of teams for real impact*. New York, NY: The Free Press.

Appendix B. Tall Objectives Closer Up

As I've said, tall objectives must have certain characteristics. They are described in more detail in the first section of this appendix. In the second section the eight attributes of one of the most important characteristics, quality, are listed.

Section 1. The Characteristics of Tall Objectives

They are Self-Owned

Teams that set their own objectives will own them. Owning them, they will thus be committed to them, and this commitment will be enhanced if the objectives possess all of the remaining characteristics.

They are Correctly Aligned

Self-ownership and self-management don't mean selfishness or seclusion. Objectives must be aligned correctly with a number of significant reference points. Otherwise, the organization would be like a loose canon shooting out objectives and follow-through efforts in random directions. Needless to say, the organization's values and direction both long term (vision and strategic plan) and short term (annual goals) are major reference points. The marketplace is another, and considerations of it would be reflected in the company's direction and in more specific determinations of consumer expectations. Objectives must also be aligned with suppliers of any resources needed to help achieve the objectives. Finally, objectives need to be aligned among and within the teams in light of any interdependencies and to avoid conflicts and redundancies.

They are Ethically and Environmentally Responsible

Ignoble objectives must be staunchly avoided. They are the ones that can only be met by unethical behavior, or require pursuit of results knowingly harmful to others or the environment, or knowingly lead to results that are inferior (I discuss the ethical imperative of quality in a moment). It takes moral grit to stick to noble objectives in the face of stiff competition or otherwise tough times (as I said earlier, principled MBR is not for wimps). But ethically besting a competitor is not ignoble. It's capitalism at its finest.

Objectives must also be stated honestly. An example of a dishonest objective would be one that deliberately understates a target so that it can be easily exceeded, thereby possibly garnering more recognition and reward for the person (s) who exceeded it. I have seen this happen many times.

They are Clear and Specific

One MBO author has written that "objectives may range from general 'fuzzies' to specific goals, with the fuzzies (borrowing an example from that author, "increase our share of the market") being a starting point to getting to the specific goals (again borrowing from that author, "50,000 units of product A sold by the end of this year").[1] Personally, I think that encouraging fuzzies could start a bad habit of fuzziness. I have seen many fuzzy objectives however fuzzier may have been their conception. Better, I believe, to start and end with clear and optimally specific objectives so that there are no misunderstandings and so that performance can be tracked and appraised without any uncertainties.

Note that I said "optimally specific" but didn't qualify clarity. An objective can never be too clear, but it can be too specific. An objective needs to specify whatever features of quality, efficiency, and timeliness are desired without going into unnecessary and numbing details (for example, reducing overall cost by X amount might be specific enough, while including requirements for component costs might add too much detail and go beyond the what into the how). While research has shown that specific objectives motivate people more than do general goals, it seems to me that overly specific ones will be burdensome, uninspiring, and unreceptive to creativity and serendipty.[2]

They are Change-Oriented and Changeable

Heraclitus, the Greek philosopher, observed more than 2500 years ago that, "Nothing is more permanent than change." Today is much different. Change still keeps happening, of course, but the pace of it happening would spin the Greek's head. Change comes so fast now that there is little time to prepare for it or to recover from it if one is unprepared. It's like changing a tire on a speeding car. What this means is that, contrary to the classical MBO literature, and with the possible exception of the continuing responsibilities associated with extra roles such as "secretary/treasurer," there can be no such thing as "routine" objectives, or objectives for "routine" or "maintenance" operations.[3] A "routine" expectation and operation will be left in the dust with Heraclitus. So whatever an objective targets, the target better not be the target of last year. The objective better target something that is newer or better in some way. Moreover, because change marches on (no, make that races ahead), objectives need to be changeable at anytime during the performance year if changes in the situation demand it.

They are Quality-Oriented

Recall that results targeted in an objective can vary on four dimensions, or criteria. Quality of results (the "how well" dimension) is the only one of the four that must always be targeted. If it is not, the objective cannot pretend to be tall. Even if the objective is to make a product or provide a service in a cheaper price range, the objective must be quality oriented. Why should anyone have to pay for shoddy products and services?

Two imperatives demand quality and nothing less. One is an ethical imperative. Quality is its own virtue. To quote one corporate executive, "we are morally obligated to produce quality."[4] What is the basis for that obligation? Recall the ethical value of excellence. The Greek philosophers equated quality with the ideal of excellence.[5] The biblical writers also valued excellence. I spotted over 50 references to it in the King James Version, such as this one: "Seek that ye may excell."[6] It would also be less responsible to do less than one's best at work for the benefit of others (investors and customers, for example) regardless of whether they expect it.

The other imperative is an economic one. A company known for its superior products or services has a competitive advantage. And quality is not too costly to achieve because it's cheaper to avoid mistakes. It has even been argued, perhaps with some exaggeration, that "quality is not just free; it's better than free."[7] However, a quality focus must not become a compulsion in the midst of changing technologies and markets. There is no future in continuously improving a buggy whip.

To target quality, one has to know what it is. One view is that quality must have every one of eight attributes or dimensions. They are listed and briefly defined in the second section of this appendix. The most common view is that quality is whatever the customer expects. While customer expectations obviously are important, four qualifications need to be added to the "customer is always right" dictum.

One is that the customer is not always right. I know from personal experience. Starting out very young in the retail business, the dictum was drilled into me by my father and another successful businessman. As I matured and gained more experience, I realized that customers are sometimes wrong and sometimes a pain in the butt, and when they are they should not be patronizingly treated as if they were right and pleasant. Many times later when I was writing proposals for prospective customers, I had to tell them that they had misconceived their problem and needed a different solution than what they were seeking. I won my share of contracts with this educate-the-prospect approach.

The second qualification is that if customers are the sole benchmark, the temptation to dupe and exploit them must be avoided. I once read in a consumer magazine that a manufacturer sought to cut costs by making a gradually inferior product on the gamble that unsophisticated customers would not notice the difference because the product was already a complex piece of equipment! That is both an unethical and foolishly shortsighted tactic.

Thirdly, the dictum implicitly discourages going beyond customers' expectations and most definitely inhibits going outside of them. Going outside of them is my definition of inventiveness, a hallmark of progress. How could customers expect desktop computers before they were even invented? And thank goodness they were so that I was able to write this book using one instead of my old typewriter that is sentimentally stored in the attic.

Fourthly, the very essence of quality is intrinsic to it and may escape the customer's point of view. The ideal of excellence comes closest I think to that essence. But it would be disastrous to embrace this ideal and ignore the customer's viewpoint. For even after having not ignored it, the typical company is still likely to lose 20% of its customers annually.[8] In targeting quality, therefore, it seems eminently prudent to add the more vague but ethically right ideal to the more practical criterion of customer expectations. This approach enables the product maker or service provider to stay attuned to the marketplace while still heeding the advice of the great inventor, Thomas Edison, that "there is a better way to everything; find it."

They May Also Target Quantity, Cost, and Timeliness

Depending on the circumstances, an objective may need to specify one or more of the three remaining criteria. They are quantity ("how many"), cost ("how much"), and timeliness ("how soon"). Quantity could be critical, for example, if there were a large demand for the product or service. Cost reduction could be critical, for example, if the company found itself being undercut by its competitors. Timeliness, too, could be critical, such as when being first to the market with new products is a strategic priority. Ordinarily, timeliness is included in all objectives so as not to leave them dangling or open-ended. Masterpieces in progress can be an exception to this rule of thumb, however. Michelangelo, the great Italian sculptor, painter, architect, and poet took 10 years to paint the Sistine Chapel. Every once in awhile during that time the Pope would ask him when his work would be finished. "When I'm done," he would always answer.

They are Track-Able and Appraisable

Objectives must specify observable or measurable conditions of results so that progress toward their achievement can be tracked and their actual achievement can be determined. The conditions, also known as indicators, are expressed in terms of the criteria already mentioned. A "fully loaded" objective would specify particular conditions of quality, quantity, cost, and timeliness to be expected.

The familiar adage, "what gets measured gets done," tends to spawn excessive measurement that gets in the way of getting things done. Excessive requirements for "counting and clocking" need to be avoided in specifying the conditions. Some observable conditions may not even need to be measured, let alone with any precision. Consider aesthetics. An aesthetically pleasing product is usually one of its important conditions, but one that may not need to be measured at all even if it could be measured at all. Seeing the product may be sufficient. I have seen first-hand some of Michelangelo's masterpieces and was absolutely awed by them. Measuring the quality of his work would be ridiculous. On a more mundane matter, neither is measurement necessary to tell me that I hear a very annoying transformer hum in a relatively new microwave oven.

They are Tough but Doable

To stay in business and to keep performers motivated, tall objectives need to be tough but doable. An objective would not be a tall one if it weren't challenging. But if the challenge is unrealistic, then the objective is too tough and probably undoable. Only Alpine objectives should reach for the sky.

Section 2. More on Quality

According to an award-winning author, every product must have eight attributes of quality for its maker to stay competitive.[9]They are:

- Performance
- Features
- Reliability
- Conformance
- Durability
- Serviceability
- Aesthetics
- Perceived Quality

Performance refers to the intended function of the product or service (e.g., if the product is a boat, it stays afloat and moves efficiently while in the water).

Features are accessories intended to enhance or expand performance (the boat has lockable compartments).

Reliability is dependability (lapse of time before boat repairs are needed).

Conformance refers to fidelity to company specifications (whether the boat meets all of its maker's requirements).

Durability is an extension of reliability and refers to the product's life span (lapse of time before the boat's irrevocable failure).

Serviceability refers to economy of maintenance (boat repair costs).

Aesthetics are in the eyes, ears, and feel of the beholder (whether the boat's motor runs quietly enough).

Perceived quality refers to the customer's overall judgment of excellence (whether the customer would buy the boat if starting over) and, it seems to me, comes close to the quality ideal while still leaving room for the possibility of achieving even greater quality independently of the customer (by adding, for example, a surprise feature at no extra cost).

NOTES AND REFERENCES FOR APPENDIX B

1. Albrecht, K. (1978). *Successful management by objectives: An action manual.* Englewood Cliffs, NJ: Prentice-Hall, Inc., p. 74.
2. Huszczo, GE. (1996). *Tools for team excellence: Getting your team into high gear and keeping it there.* Palo Alto, CA: Davies-Black Publishing.
3. Odiorne, GS. (1979). *MBO II.* Belmont CA: Fearon Pitman Publishers, Inc., p 127.
4. Step, LS. (1991, March 31). In search of ethics. *The Washinton Post,* H1,4.
5. Reeves, CA. & Bednar, DA. (1994). Defining quality: Alternatives and implications. *Academy of Management Review,* 19, 419-445.
6. 1st. Corinthians, 28:29.
7. Skrzycki, C. (1988, October 2). The quest for the best: U.S. firms turn to quality as competitive tool. *The Washington Post,* H2-3.
8. Hope, T. & Hope, J. (1995). *Transforming the bottom line: Managing performance by the numbers.* Boston, MA: Harvard Business School Press.
9. Garwin, DA. (1987). Competing on the eight dimensions of quality. *Harvard Business Review,* 87, 101-109.

Appendix C. How To Create And Use Examples Of Short Behaviors

This appendix with its five sections is meant to show how examples of short behaviors can be created, publicized, and used in a company. The first tells how to create examples. The second illustrates some examples that could be drawn upon by an ad hoc team to make its task easier. The third provides some negative verbs that might help the team think of more examples if more are needed. The fourth suggests how to publicize the examples created by the team so as not to accentuate the negative. The fifth suggests how to use the examples whenever needed in the course of managing performance.

Section 1. How to Create Examples

Step 1. Confirm Technical Competencies

Technical or functional competencies are of two kinds, core and ancillary. At the core are the knowledge, skills, and abilities essential for performing the primary operations of the business (e.g., the microchip processing of the computer maker). Without the core competencies, there would be no business. The ancillary competencies are the knowledge, skills, and abilities necessary to perform work such as planning, budgeting, marketing and the like that support the core business.

The reason for confirming the competencies is that they provide the backdrop for creating examples of incompetent behaviors. The competencies can be confirmed through already available information such as the company's selection criteria, training and operating manuals, and the roles and responsibilities of people throughout the organization.

This step doesn't need to deal with behaviors reflecting interpersonal incompetence. They should emerge naturally in doing the next two steps.

Step 2. Describe Behavioral Incidents

Incidents are one-step removed from examples to be put on the list because incidents are more specific, usually describing the short behaviors involved in more detail and usually within the context of situations. Incidents would be too specific and impractical to use instead of examples but are helpful to draw upon in creating the examples. I find that it's usually better when processing information to go from the specific to the general so that one can see whether useful information would be lost in going to the next level of generality. Less specific examples if preferred can then be extracted from the incidents once the latter have been described.

This step begins with team members individually or collectively writing down incidents involving the different competency areas, both technical and interpersonal, and also a variety of unmotivated and unethical behaviors. The incidents may be real as well as ones that could happen at work.

Asking leading questions will help get the team started. Here are three sample questions: "What were the behaviors involved the last time someone poorly performed a technical function or skill required?" "When someone really irritated the other team members, what did the person actually do to irritate them?" "When someone acted unethically, what did the person do?" If there is any doubt about whether an incident involves an unethical behavior, the "conscience-checking questions" listed in Appendix E are a useful cross-reference.

Members should stop writing incidents only after no more can be recalled, or imagined as being possible at work.

Step 3. Create Examples

The team should start its list by extracting behavioral examples from the incidents. The team will need to decide how specific or general to make the examples. I would recommend more general ones. More specific examples make the list longer and not any more useful. When a specific incident of short behavior occurs at work, it will probably be recognized immediately as a short behavior, and it shouldn't be difficult to find where it's represented on the list of more generalized examples. For instance, you'll see a generalized example in Section 2 on "mismanages own performance." This, of course, summarizes a variety of more specific actions, such as, say, falsifying one's self-appraisal. The team may or may not decide to include in the final list more specific examples of all possible ways to mismanage performance.

The extracted examples should represent as much as possible the kinds of incompetent, unmotivated, and unethical behaviors that have happened or could happen at work in the company and that would be problematical or intolerable either happening once, repetitively, or as part of an over-all pattern. The behavioral examples extracted need to be compared against the competencies, the examples in Section 2 that I've provided, and the ethical values identified in Chapter 1(accountability, altruism, excellence, fairness and justice, honesty and integrity, loyalty, promise keeping, respecting others, and responsibility) to see if there would be any substantial under-representation in the final list. If there would be, Sections 2 and 3 may be useful in providing ideas for more examples.

If the team has created a large number of examples, the final list would be easier to use if the examples were subdivided into smaller categories. This can be done by putting the examples on index cards and then sorting them into categories of similar content. Sorting the examples will also help highlight redundant examples that could be culled. More importantly, though, the team may decide to summarize a category of very similar or related examples and put only the summarized example on the list.

Flagging Certain Examples. Before making the list final, the ad hoc team should flag those examples that represent behaviors that if they occur once (e.g., a serious blunder, an egregiously unethical action, etc.) would definitely require formal documentation and possibly some form of intervention such as a rescue effort or a penalty. These would be behaviors such as serious blunders and egregiously unethical transgressions (see Appendix E for a "conscience-checking" guide on determining conduct that would be unethical). Other short behaviors may be given some slack (we are, after all, not perfect, so some leeway on our more innocuous imperfections should be allowed). Consider abrasive behaviors, for instance. They might be tolerated on occasion but not, perhaps, if they become a persistent pattern.

Section 2. Some Illustrative Examples

I've put into this section some illustrative examples of short behaviors that the ad hoc team may wish to consider borrowing from as it creates its own list. The examples are grouped into a few categories that are probably not mutually exclusive. There are no examples of incompetent behaviors in purely technical functions (e.g., inept processing of computer chips) that represent the particular technology of the business. So the team will have to generate its own examples in order to reflect the technical competencies required.

A. Examples of Some Short Behaviors in Planning, Decision-Making, and Problem-Solving

Focuses unduly on short-term considerations.
Belittles planning efforts.
Fails to consider all necessary factors when planning ahead.
Doesn't allocate and schedule resources to assure their availability by priority.
Fails to anticipate problems before they happen.
Doesn't anticipate and capitalize on important changes affecting the work.
Rarely uses most useful data in decision-making.
Makes rash decisions.
Procrastinates in making decisions or taking necessary action.
Draws premature conclusions.
Overly simplifies complex issues.
Overly complicates simple issues.
Acts impulsively.
Doesn't ask the right questions to properly size up a problem.
Doesn't recognize when a problem is critical enough to require immediate attention.
Wants to put off badly needed changes.
Looks for quick fixes.
Treats symptoms rather than causes.
Misjudges strengths or weaknesses.
Makes faulty assumptions.
Collects too much data.
Gets weighted down by paralysis of analysis.
Gets bogged down in unnecessary details.
Wants to play it safe rather than venture forward.
Dismisses new ideas out of hand.
Lets new opportunities slip away.

Communicates in unclear and vague terms.

B. Examples of Some Other Short Behaviors

<u>Loafing/Shirking Responsibility/Lack of Teamwork</u>

Doesn't give commitment to personally disliked decisions.
Doesn't follow through on commitments or promises.
Avoids extra tasks and responsibilities.
Tries to unload work on others.
Pleads ignorance to avoid responsibility.
Generally looks for the easier work.
Prolongs tasks to appear busy.
Slackens up when more rather than less effort is needed.
Wastes time unless constantly prodded.
Intentionally works slow or procrastinates.
Doesn't pitch in to help others when they need and want it.
Resents being asked to help.
Cooperates only when asked.
Keeps to one self when it's inappropriate.
Doesn't look out for the welfare of the team.
Shrinks from unpleasant but necessary tasks.
Tends to give up if problems occur.
Tries to improve performance only when prodded to do so.
Makes only sporadic attempts to keep abreast of new and related developments.
Never asks for help if unsure of something or if errors are made.
Puts personal interest first to the detriment of the job.
Uses slow periods to do personal business.
Unjustifiably tries to take on others' responsibilities.
Disparages ideas of others.
Doesn't respect differences of opinion.
Promotes own personal view.
Stubbornly persists in advancing own views on a matter.
Refuses to consider viable alternatives or behaves in other inflexible ways.
Fails to consult with others when necessary.
Insists on having own way.
Resents not getting own way.
Insists he/she is always right.
Refuses to explain own actions, expecting others to simply accept them.

Interpersonally Abrasive Behaviors

Keeps others waiting unnecessarily.
Doesn't return phone calls or e-mails.
Boasts about own actions and accomplishments.
Reacts defensively to criticism and suggestions.
Resists or rejects valid feedback about own behavior or ideas.
Provides ready excuses or blames others for own shortcomings.
Gives feedback in a non-constructive manner.
Gives vague, unhelpful feedback.
Takes credit undeservedly.
Tries to coerce others into agreement or into taking a point of view or action.
Tries to suppress or smooth over disagreements to avoid conflicts.
Brings up petty or irrelevant issues.
Stirs up dissension.
Makes unreasonable requests.
Does little things to make it unpleasant to be a member of the team.
Makes insensitive remarks or in other ways acts insensitively or rudely.
Acts in irritating ways.
Acts impatiently with others.
Shows outbursts of temper.
Argues needlessly.
Monopolizes conversations and meetings.
Interrupts people.
Doesn't listen to others.
Wants to take action before agreement is reached.
Rushes others unnecessarily or unreasonably.
Sulks when unhappy about what is happening.
Criticizes persons rather than their ideas or performance.
Criticizes others behind their backs.
Openly criticizes others in public.
Talks about others derogatorily.
Gets into needless arguments with others.
Holds grudges.

Other Short Behaviors, Including Unethical Ones

Lets little things bother him or her.
Overreacts emotionally even in small crises.
Mismanages own performance.
Deliberately withholds information or help.
Only tells the real reasons for own actions when useful to do so.
Pays lip service to principles and decisions.
Says one thing and then does another.
Spreads unfounded, negative rumors.

Divulges confidential information.
Pries into other person's personal affairs
Conceals own mistakes.
Makes misleading statements.
Gives evasive answers.
Fabricates statements or answers.
Uses indirect, manipulative means to influence others.
Conceals own motives under some pretense.
Plays budget games (e.g., overstates funds needed).
Manipulates data/reports to make them look more favorable.
Rationalizes wrongdoing (e.g., by trivializing its significance).
Uses loopholes to circumvent legal requirements.
Doesn't hesitate to act ruthlessly when expedient.
Treats others only as means to own ends.
Uses slow periods to do personal business.
Misuses privileges.
Knowingly creates badvantages.
Makes personal use of company equipment and supplies.
Looks the other way on wrongdoing.
Verbally harasses others.
Curses people.
Plays mean pranks on others.
Engages in horseplay.
Bills the company for personal expenses.
Disparages or smears competitors when dealing with customers.
Knowingly announces products or services prematurely to stem loss of customers.
Woos customers with questionable price discounting.
Low-balls bids.
Proffers or accepts gratuities where law allows.
Uses deceptive or other improper tactics to acquire information about competitors.
Uses hard sell techniques.
Doesn't disclose that a product guarantee is conditional.
Exaggerates claims of products/services.
Plays on customers' fears or guilt to sell them products or services.
Markets cheaper products/services to people with lower incomes.
Refuses to trade in a low-income area.
Accepts entertainment offers or other favors in return for business.
Leaks negative information about competitors to the press.
Uses legal but questionable pressure tactics to stifle competition.

Illegal Behaviors[1]

Steals money of other belongings of others, including the embezzling of funds.
Receives stolen property.
Destroys property.
Transacts in stolen items.

Trespasses (e.g., on a competitor's secured property).
Extorts, including blackmailing, by force, threat, or any other means.
Takes kickbacks.
Offers, gives, solicits, or receives bribes or gratuities.
Appropriates copyrights or trademarks.
Pays or receives unauthorized compensation.
Unlawfully makes, traffics in, possesses, or uses controlled substances or goods.
Engages in, aids, or abets racketeering.
Falsifies or conceals facts related to legal documents or inquiries.
Defrauds or deceives victims in business dealings, including advertising.
Discriminates or intimidates to interfere with an individual's civil rights.
Invades others' rightful privacy.
Unlawfully deals with goods or other materials harmful to the public.
Endangers the public through degradation of the environment.
Riggs bids.
Fixes prices.
Makes market-allocation agreements with competitors.
Engages in monetary transactions linked to unlawful activities.

Section 3. Some Negative Verbs

A negative verb is the most abbreviated form of a short behavior. Stand-alone verbs may be helpful in stimulating further thinking when needed in writing either incidents or examples of short behavior. I've prepared a list of verbs simply by going through a standard dictionary. I've eliminated many verbs by trying to avoid synonyms and to minimize duplication of the verbs used in the examples of the previous section. Also excluded are extremely negative and unnecessary verbs, such as "kill."

Abuse	Affront	Agitate	Alienate	Aggravate	Anger
Badger	Bamboozle	Belittle	Besmirch	Betray	Bluster
Boar	Bother	Bully	Bungle	Cheapen	Clutter
Complicate	Crash	Dally	Deface	Defame	Degrade
Derail	Desert	Destroy	Diminish	Disappoint	Disgrace
Disgust	Dismay	Distract	Disturb	Embitter	Endanger
Exasperate	Finagle	Flounder	Forget	Foul	Fumble
Goad	Hamper	Hamstring	Harangue	Hinder	Impose
Impugn	Insinuate	Interfere	Intimidate	Inveigh	Inveigle
Jeer	Lapse	Lie	Loaf	Lose	Machinate
Malign	Malinger	Mar	Misadvise	Mis	Mope
Nag	Needle	Offend	Overact	Over	Pad
Pester	Pique	Plod	Pollute	Pontificate	Rankle
Revile	Scoff	Scorn	Slight	Slur	Spite
Spoil	Stall	Strut	Stultify	Stumble	Stupefy
Tamper	Tease	Traumatize	Trick	Trifle	Unsettle
Upset	Usurp	Waste	Weaken	Worry	Wreck

Section 4. How to Publicize the Examples

Once the team is satisfied it has enough examples, they should be put into a handbook that is given to everyone in the company. It should be made clear there that the examples are illustrative only, that they don't exhaust all possibilities, and that not finding any examples resembling an actual occurrence doesn't necessarily mean a short behavior hasn't occurred. Common sense judgment should suffice in such cases to determine whether the actual behavior constitutes a negative manner of performance. And as I've already mentioned, when the question is one of the ethics of an action, referring to the conscience-checking" questions in Appendix E should be helpful in making a determination.

So as to accentuate the positive, the predominant theme of the handbook should be about tall performance, not short performance. The handbook should thus have in it a lot of other material besides the list. It could have a section on the company's vision and values. It could also stress the importance of setting and achieving tall objectives and perhaps discuss what makes up tall objectives. And in introducing the list, the handbook should emphasize that everyone in the company is both trusted and expected to keep their manner of performance positive and that the list need only be referred to when exceptions arise.

When given a personal copy of the handbook, each person could be asked to sign in it a pledge to commit to tall performance. As part of the screening process in hiring new members, applicants could be shown the handbook and asked if they would be willing to sign the pledge if hired. Pledges are one of the first opportunities members have to express a commitment to the way the company goes about its business. Pledges by themselves, of course, can be relatively meaningless without further opportunities through the performance management process to back up words with real performance.

Section 5. How to Use the Examples

The most important purpose of the examples has already been fulfilled in just creating and publicizing them. That purpose is the establishment and communication of organizational norms about behavior. Norms can have a powerful influence on how people behave in an organization, and in this case, how not to behave. But there is also a secondary purpose to the examples, and that is providing a frame of reference that may be useful on occasion when managing performance.

When Setting Tall Expectations. I don't think the handbook and its examples need to be reviewed at the beginning of each and every performance year? To require such a periodic review risks insulting peoples' intelligence and is probably unnecessary anyway. People reviewed the examples when given the handbook, know that tall expectations doesn't call for short behaviors, and know that the examples can always be referred to whenever it would be useful to do so.

When Tending Performance. Tending performance obviously should focus on any specific behaviors that require attention, but the examples, especially the flagged ones, might be a helpful reference if there are any doubts about whether the actual behaviors really warrant attention or there is resistance to giving them attention.

<u>When Appraising Manner of Performance</u>. When people in an organization are capable of and committed to tall performance, and it has been managed well, "Yes" will probably be the truthful answer to the appraisal question: Manner of performance consistently positive? Here are two criteria to consider in determining if that should be the answer:

- Consider manner of performance to have been consistently positive unless—
    - it was represented by any example (s) of flagged behaviors or,
    - formal attention required regardless of any flagged or other examples

The first criterion obviously shouldn't be used alone because it's always possible that a truly negative manner of performance won't resemble any of the examples of short behaviors in the handbook. But even if there is a resemblance, it shouldn't override available information on the actual manner of performance and common sense in using that information in determining a final appraisal.

The occurrence of any actual behaviors that required a rescue effort doesn't necessarily preclude a positive appraisal. It might still be justified if the effort succeeded without involving a long and costly undertaking. Moreover, people should be afforded some leniency and given the benefit of any doubts when certifying their self-appraisals.

<u>When Sanctioning Performance</u>. The examples can be helpful in developing a general guide on punishable behaviors. The guide should have two parts, one for examples of punishable behaviors and the other for recommended penalties for the different kinds of behaviors. The groundwork for the first part has already been done in that examples of punishable behaviors have already been flagged.

Before appropriate penalties can be suggested, the level of harmfulness or costliness of the behavioral examples needs to be estimated. This is a much more important consideration in choosing appropriate penalties than is the frequency of the offensive behavior. A frequently repeated minor infraction can never reach the level of harmfulness of an extremely grave infraction. Nevertheless, frequency obviously shouldn't be ignored or tolerated if it becomes a real issue.

Three levels of harmfulness/costliness ought to be sufficient to help determine the appropriate penalty; namely, less serious, more serious, and illegal. The first two cover both wrong-do and won't do behaviors. For illegal offenses, obviously, legal authorities will weigh in with their own determinations.

Here are some questions the elaborated answers to which will help differentiate among the three levels:

- What was the actual behavior?
- Which if any ethical values breeched?
- Was a law violated?
- Exactly what harm done or cost incurred?
- Who and how many people/organizations harmed?
- Financial, physical, psychological nature of harm done?
- Company's reputation jeopardized or tarnished?
- Customers/suppliers alienated/lost?
- Media attention?
- Monetary value of harm/cost can be estimated?
- Remedy available to undo harm/cost?
- Cost to organization of remedy?
- Remorsefulness shown?
- Offer to help on a remedy?
- Has the behavior occurred before and what was the response to it?
- How likely is the behavior to recur?

Note that only the last two questions relate to frequency of the offensive behavior. The rest relate to the nature of the behavior's consequences.

Flagged examples from the handbook or actual incidents can be used as a frame of reference in defining the different levels by tying answers to them. For example, fighting on the premises might be labeled "legal/more serious." The definitions can be refined in any subsequent revisions of the guide as experiences with them accumulate.

Once the levels are operationally defined, suggested penalties need to be listed for each level. The kinds of penalties available need to be brainstormed first. Then, different penalties need to be recommended for each level of harmfulness/cost. Penalties for the most harmful/costly level should be considered first. For example, dismissal ought to be suggested for the most serious legal and illegal offenses (but, of course, with actual dismissal awaiting the outcome of due process if it's invoked). Then penalties for lesser offenses should be considered. It's helpful to ask in considering a specific penalty for a given level of offenses whether the penalty would be perceived as being reasonably less than penalties for offenses at a more serious level and reasonably more than penalties for offenses at a less serious level.

NOTE AND REFERENCE FOR APPENDIX C

1. I'm not a lawyer, so I drew the broad examples of illegal behaviors from the US Sentencing Commission Guidelines Manual, November 1, 1991.

Appendix D. A Resource Guide For Rescuing Falling Performance

This appendix is an annotated bibliography on a few selected readings about troubleshooting and rescuing falling performance. There are thousands of published discourses on the subject-some 2000 books just on coaching alone. So out there is an immense body of knowledge, a tremendous resource. Think of an annotated bibliography, even one as short as this one, as a fast way for performance consultants among teams to tap a bit of that resource. My bibliography over-represents coaching as an intervention, but at least all 2000 books don't need to be read, and coaching is a very cost-effective way to respond quickly to many short behaviors.

Axelrod, A. & Holtje, J. (1997). *201 ways to deal with difficult people.* New York: McGraw-Hill.

This book is suitable for performance consultants in tall, medium, and short organizations since the difficult people (e.g., tyrants, loafers, braggarts) include bosses, colleagues, and subordinates. While unduly pessimistic about the chance of changing the way these people behave, the authors' practical advice goes beyond just learning how to tolerate them to learning how to respond in ways that could possibly change their behaviors, at least temporarily in interactions where the advice is followed.

Ackroyd, S. & Thompson, P. (1999). *Organizational misbehavior.* Thousand Oaks, CA: Sage.

Although my published review of this very academic book was critical (*Personnel Psychology, in press*), it's not without its redeeming features. Recall the physics imperative for empowerment. I got that idea mostly from the book's documentation of the reciprocating escalation of resistance by labor and control by management. While there are some very funny anecdotes about horseplay, sexual misconduct, and other misbehaviors, reading this abstract ought to be enough to reinforce the argument that management from above can beget more of the very actions it's trying to stop.

Banner, RW. (2000). *Team troubleshooter: How to find and fix problems.* Palo Alto, CA: Davies-Black Publishing.

I usually am wary about testimonials on a book's cover, but in this case I concur with one of them that the "book is to be used, not just read." The author argues that, "teams are their own best problem solvers," and instead of relying on outside experts should use his book (naturally). That's quiet a boast, but he delivers. He suggests starting out by completing his diagnostic tool, the "Team Health Check." The answers direct the team to one or more problem-fixing tools. For example, if the team is "stuck in a rut" and needs to be more innovative, it's directed to six tools and instructions to get it out of the rut. I strongly recommend this book for performance consultants, and it wouldn't be a bad idea if all team members read it, too.

Cavaiola, AA. & Lavender, NJ. (2000). *Toxic co-workers: How to deal with dysfunctional people on the job.* Oakland, CA: New Harbinger Publications, Inc.

Believe me, the people portrayed in this book really are dysfunctional (e.g., borderline neurotics), but aren't, the authors claim, all that uncommon in the workplace. Although the authors are clinical psychologists, this is a readable, self-help book. However, the self-help is mainly aimed at reducing the stress of the people who have to work with the toxics. Well, come to think of it, any help that would do that would be helpful.

Dotlich, DL. & Cairo, PC. (1999). *Action coaching: How to leverage individual performance for company success.* San Francisco, CA: Jossey-Bass.

Action coaching leads to actions by those coached to change their behaviors through self-awareness, increased motivation, and guidance. The authors recommend peer coaches in flatter organizations of self-managed teams and point out that it doesn't take "coaching school" to be a coach. Eight steps of coaching are outlined and explained. Tips are offered on how to coach a variety of difficult people (e.g., egotists, team wreckers). Also included in the book is a short but good discussion of role- playing, a useful exercise to include when the target of coaching are interpersonal and attitudinal problems.

Fisher, K. & Belgard, W. (1995). *Tips for teams: A ready reference for solving common team problems.* New York: McGraw-Hill.

I really like this book. The problems presented are indeed common and run the gamut of those any team, whether self-managed or managed from above, will encounter at some time during their lifespan (although, some of those problems wouldn't be so common if the We/Me model were followed). A number of helpful tips and resources are provided for solving each problem. For example, if team confusion is the problem, part of the authors' advice is to get rid of rules and use principles. Amen!

Fried, NE. (1990). *Outrageous conduct: Bizarre behavior at work.* Dublin, OH: Intermediaries Press.

The book is full of true vignettes of short behaviors on the outer fringe (e.g., "flagrant fellatio") compiled by the author, who then had a panel of experts (e.g., a director of employee relations, employment law specialists) read them and offer their advice on how the incidents should have best been handled. While the author's approach is clever, I think the book is of limited value, perhaps more suited to dealing with outrageous conduct in hierarchies.

Herbelin, S. & Guiney, P. (Eds.). (1998). *The do's and don'ts of work team coach: A comprehensive study of the worker/coach interpersonal relationship.* Riverbank, CA: Herbelin Publishing.

To be honest with you, I haven't read this little book, but the reviews of it are very compelling. The do's and don'ts are written from the perspective of the people coached. If I were a team member who had taken on the extra role of performance consultant, I'd certainly consider reading and using this book.

Hollands, JA. (1997). *Red ink behaviors: Measure the surprisingly high co$t of problem behaviors in valuable employees.* Mountain View, CA: Blake/Madsen.

What a catchy phrase, "red ink behaviors." It was enough to lure me into asking my book review editor to send me the book to review. My review turned out more negative than positive (*Personnel Psychology*, 1998, 51, 519-522). One of the positives is that the author's "costimator," while worse than fuzzy math, nevertheless clearly shows how valuable employees can be costly in their manner of performance. Another positive is that the author's approach to coaching such people looks sound and seems to work (alert the person to the costly behaviors, have the person practice alternative behaviors, get the person to announce the efforts to change, get others to support the efforts, and continue the coaching until the new behaviors are established).

Hudson, FM. (1999). *The handbook of coaching: A comprehensive resource guide for managers, executives, consultants, and human resource professionals.* San Francisco, CA: Jossey-Bass.

My annotated bibliography contains only a few books on coaching. A prominent feature of Hudson's book is that its annotated bibliography is nearly 150 pages! It's a veritable mother lode. You can be sure I'd mine it if I were a performance consultant.

Huszczo, GE. (1996). *Tools for team excellence: Getting your team into high gear and keeping it that way.* Palo Alto, CA: Davies-Black Publishing.

The author of this very practical book for teams believes that a systematic approach to problem solving may be the most important procedure for a team to have (personally, I would put MBR first). After reviewing many approaches described in the literature, the author developed a four-step model and has been successfully training hundreds of teams on how to use it. The first step is to become aware of the problem (monitoring via the We/Me model will, of course, guarantee the aim of this first step). The second step is to analyze the problem (think about and look for all possible causes, then focus on the core causes). The last two steps are to choose a solution from among several considered and then to implement that solution.

Langdon, DG. et al. (Eds). (1999). *Intervention resource guide: 50 performance improvement tools.* San Francisco, CA: Jossey-Bass/Pfeiffer.

Although my published review of this book was ambivalent (*Personnel Psychology*, 2000, 53, 785-787), recall those interventions I quickly reeled off in Chapter 6. Some of them I'd never heard of until I read this book because they came after the prime of my time. But those interventions reportedly can be effective in certain conditions. I'd recommend that any performance consultant, no matter if much younger than I, take a look at this book. Some of the tools no doubt will seem daunting, but you can always turn to the tools' authors who are mostly practicing consultants.

Solomon, M. (1999). *Working with difficult people.* Paramus, NJ: Prentice-Hall.

More difficult people-bullies, hagglers, connivers, socializers, stallers, you name it. The author offers practical advice on how to deal with three categories of them; difficult colleagues, and, true to hierarchical form, difficult bosses and difficult subordinates. The book ends with a helpful summary of 10 pointers (e.g., be straightforward, be unemotional).

Whitmore, J. (1996). *Coaching for performance: A practical guide.* London: Nicholas Bealey.

And last, only because of the author's last name, is his book. I disagree somewhat with how he conceptualizes coaching. To him, for instance, self-awareness is sensitivity to inputs, but to me it's also sensitivity to outputs. Setting concepts aside, I think he has good, practical advice to offer on how to help a person raise self-awareness and take responsibility for behavioral change, especially in the context of teams. Self-awareness and taking responsibility are, after all, attributes of being empowered.

Appendix E. Good Decisions And Good Conflict

Needless to say, empowered people make far more decisions and far more pivotal ones daily than commanded and controlled people ever make. And because decisions require making choices, conflicts are often unavoidable. In this appendix are some advice and a few suggested readings on how to make sure the decisions are good ones and on how to use conflict to advantage when it can be done so.

Section 1. Good Decisions

People committed to tall performance will always seek to make good decisions and to eschew "group-think" in the course of the decision-making in team settings. Good decisions must lead to actions aligned with the company's vision, values, mission, operational goals, and team and individual objectives. Good decisions don't lead to negative success or negative failure.

Above all, good decisions must be ethical ones. Before making any decision, therefore, these "conscience-checking" questions need to be raised if there is any doubt about the ethics of the actions the decisions would require:

- Would the action look like any of the examples of unethical behaviors?
- Would the action involve dishonesty?
- Would the action lack integrity?
- Would the action be disloyal?
- Would the action break a promise?
- Would the action be unfair?
- Would the action lack caring?
- Would the action be disrespectful?
- Would the action be a shoddy thing to do?
- Would the action be irresponsible?
- Would the action dodge accountability?
- Would the action elicit indignation or outrage?
- Need to consult others first?
- Would the action cause harm, financial, psychological, or physical?
- Would the action be illegal?
- If the action affected me or us as it might others, would I or we still do it?
- Would the action cause some sleepless nights?
- Would the action have to be rationalized?
- Would the action be embarrassing if friends knew about it?
- Mind being held accountable for the action?
- What is an ethical alternative to this action if it's unethical?

"We" think, or groupthink, as it's popularly called, is the uncritical seeking and acceptance of consensus and is definitely not the way to make good decisions. It can be just as disastrous (e.g., the Bay of Pigs fiasco) as "Me" think, or autocratic think (e.g., Napoleon's Waterloo).

Paradoxically, characteristics such as shared vision and values, which help to make teams more cohesive, also help to lead them into the trap of groupthink. Two effective techniques for not getting trapped are the use of a devil's advocate and debate in making decisions.

In using the first technique, the team first arrives at a tentative decision through some traditional process such as brainstorming or the so-called "nominal group" method in which suggestions are made individually and then ranked. A team member, or someone from another team, is then asked to play devil's advocate by criticizing the tentative decision. If the criticism is valid, the tentative decision will have to be modified or abandoned in favor of some entirely different course of action.

The use of debate is more appropriate when there is greater uncertainty about what to do and whatever decision is made will be more consequential. The approach starts the same way as with that of the devil's advocate. A tentative decision is proposed. But then, instead of criticizing it, a bona fide counterproposal is offered that is based on assumptions different from the ones underlying the tentative decision. The pros and cons of each proposal are then vigorously debated until a final decision is reached.

Section 2. Good Conflict

Not all conflict is undesirable. Conflict devoid of emotional, interpersonal wrangling can be creative and productive. The decision-making approaches I just described have constructive, non-emotional conflict deliberately programmed into them.

But what about potentially destructive conflict? The author of a book on the subject that I reviewed (*Personnel Psychology*, 1995, 48, 415-418) argues that interpersonal conflict can be avoided "almost entirely" if people within the organization treat each other as if they were important clients in a win-win rather than win-lose relationship.

Adopting that stance, of course, may sometimes be difficult to do. So the author offers an approach he claims has been highly effective in settling interpersonal disputes. It's a multi-staged one in which any subsequent stage is only used if it has to be used. In the first stage, after acknowledging and setting aside their differences, the disputants search for a common ground in order to turn the conflict into a joint problem that can be solved collaboratively. If the first stage fails, the disputants continue, but use a different approach tailored to the stage reached at the moment. The dispute is either settled or a win-lose outcome is mutually accepted.

There are many other approaches that have been promoted for resolving interpersonal conflicts. One author of a book on teams, for example, has argued that reading about what to do isn't as effective as simply learning through trial and error what to do. That may be true, but I would still recommend that one or more performance consultants among the teams review the body of knowledge on the subject and then recommend trying out one or more approaches.

Section 3. Some Suggested Readings

Alper, S. et al. (2000). Conflict management, efficacy, and performance in organizational teams. *Personnel Psychology*, 53, 625-642.

Carr, C. (1992). *Teampower: Lessons from America's top companies on putting team power to work.* Englewood Cliffs, NJ: Prentice Hall.

Crawley, J. (1995). *Constructive conflict management: Managing to make a difference.* London: Nicholas Bealey Publishing.

Isenhart, MW. & Spangle, M. (2000). *Collaborative approaches to resolving conflict.* Thousands Oaks, CA: Sage.

Kaye, K. (1994). *Workplace wars and how to avoid them: Turning personal conflicts into productive teamwork.* Chicago: AMACOM. This is the book I reviewed for the professional journal.

Robbins, H. & Finley, M. (1995). *Why teams don't work: What went wrong and how to make it right.* Princeton, NJ: Petersons'/Pacesetter Books.

Scholtes, PR. (1988). *The team handbook.* Madison, WI: Joiner Associates.

Yeatts, DF. & Hyten, C. (1998). *High-performing self-managed teams: A comparison of theory to practice.* Thousand Oaks, CA: Sage.

Crosier, RA. & Schwenk, CR. (1990). Agreement and thinking alike: Ingredients for poor decisions. *Academy of Management Journal*, 4, 69-74.

Gary B. Brumback

Appendix F. The History Of MBR

I've mentioned that the We/Me model of MBR for shorter organizations has an ironic history of predecessors in taller organizations, some of the tallest in the world. That history is highlighted here to give you an idea of just how different from the We/Me model those predecessors were and to demonstrate the overall flexibility of MBR as a process for managing performance in organizations. [1]

Section 1. MBR in the Land of Tall Giants

The Original MBR. When I was working for a not-for-profit research firm, I won a tough bidding war among competing firms for the right to develop a new selection system and a new performance appraisal system for county extension service (CES) agents working throughout the US (the bureaucracy was under a court order to develop systems that would not deny agents their equal opportunities). These agents are professionals at the grass-roots level of a vast bureaucracy comprised of the US Department of Agriculture in partnership with the 50 States and their land-grant colleges and counties. Not only did I go on to develop the systems, but I also developed a lasting fondness and appreciation for the CES and its people. To this day, I call my county's extension office when I need advice on house, lawn, and garden matters.

One of the contract requirements was to make sure the new performance appraisal system would be compatible with the front-end planning system used by the agents. That system was MBO. At the outset, I knew little about MBO, other than it neglects behaviors of work. I knew more than enough about behavioral performance appraisal, which neglects the results of work. Necessity being the mother of invention, I merged the two systems together. Voila! The first MBR was born, although at the very beginning I didn't call it MBR because the acronym had yet to occur to me, so I mistakenly called it MBO.[2]

Since I was relatively new to MBO, I was able to take a fresh look at it and come up with some new and workable changes. One feature I introduced was the weighting of objectives so that their relative importance or contribution could be taken into account in appraising and rewarding performance. Each objective was weighted in terms of four criteria.[3] The most important criterion was the nature of the change planned (agents can be thought of as change agents), and an objective could be given a base weight from 70 to 90 points depending on the kind of change planned. The three other criteria, need for, extent of, and difficulty in achieving the planned change, allowed for a few more points to be added to the base. One of the givens of the hierarchy was that agents would propose their own objectives, but their supervisors would have to approve and weight them. At the end of the performance year, agents rated their achievements on each objective using a four-level scale. Agents then submitted their self-ratings to their supervisors for review and approval.

Next, supervisors, not the agents themselves (because of policy), rated their agents' performance on six areas of work common to all agents. The first five were divided into two parts, one for rating unplanned results, one for rating behaviors. The rationale for getting ratings of unplanned results was that not all of an agent's job could be planned in advance through the setting of objectives, yet the agent should be held accountable for all results, not just those that had been targeted in objectives.

Within each of the first five areas were two sets of examples, one of results, the other of behaviors. "His/Her publicity materials have been used by other counties in the region," was one of the result examples, and "Maintains good relations with local officials and the power structure" was one of the behavioral examples for the area, "Program Promotion and Public Relations" (note that "power structure" is not a typographical error). The sixth area was labeled "Interpersonal and Personal Behaviors Generally Related to Job." Supervisors used a five-level scale to rate their agents on each and every example in all six areas.

Once the ratings were done, a "performance score" was calculated for each agent. The score was an aggregate of three component scores. One score was the product of the achievement levels and the weights of objectives. The second score was the product of the rating levels on unplanned results and the predetermined values of the examples (the examples varied in how positive or negative they were). The score for behaviors was derived in the same way as for the second score. The primary use of the performance scores was in making salary increase determinations. Before decisions could be final, supervisors' scoring and salary recommendations had to be reviewed and approved by a higher level in the hierarchy, naturally.

Following appraisal and salary administration, the last step in the process was a formal analysis by supervisors of their agents' performance to identify any deficiencies needing attention and/or any areas of potential to be developed further. A standard list of personal and situational factors and a rating scheme for assessing the factors were given to the supervisors to help them do their analyses. The personal factors were divided up into the knowledge, skills and abilities needed by agents to do their work. The situational factors were those known to complicate the agent's work whenever those factors arose. Ratings on the factors helped guide the writing of a plan of action for improving and/or developing the agent's performance.

The MBRs of US Civil Service Reform. For almost 100 years since the inception of the US civil service system, performance appraisals of civil servants from senior executives to people in the bowels of the bureaucracy had been a sham. Nearly everyone was always rated "satisfactory." Appraisals were rarely connected to planning at the beginning or to consequences at the end. Any attempt to reform the system required legislative reform. But it was the kind of obscure and unappealing problem that a long line of US presidents and legislative leaders could afford to ignore. And being generally accustomed and resigned to mediocre or worse performance from the government, taxpayers never clamored for change.

The 39th president, Jimmy Carter, however, wanted a government the people could trust to perform better. He thought reforming the civil service system would be the solution. So his administration and the Congress collaborated to create the

Civil Service Act (CSRA) in late 1978. One of its key requirements was that performance appraisal had to be reformed.

While still with the same research firm, I gave a talk to a professional association of federal personnel administrators in early 1978. I offered some suggestions on the direction I thought performance appraisal should take once the new legislation was in effect. As a result, I was asked to join the US Department of Health and Human Services (HHS), a bureaucracy so tall, massive, and far-flung that it had the reputation of being unmanageable. The Department's Assistant Secretary of Personnel Administration, Thomas McFee, was then arguably the second most influential personnel administrator in the government and had been helping the Carter administration craft the reform. He wanted his department to design its own new performance appraisal systems instead of relying on outside contractors, like I still was.

So I was faced with the option of staying a contractor in a short organization of empowered people and bidding on federal agencies requests for help (and many agencies subsequently contracted out their performance appraisal reform work) or joining one of the world's tallest organizations of mostly un- empowered people (at one time in one agency I counted 17 levels between entry-level servant and the US president). I chose the latter course because it seemed a surer opportunity for championing some of my ideas and putting them into action.

The CSRA required that new appraisal systems should start at the top with agencies' cadres of senior executives and subordinate managers. In HHS, it was decided that the department's component agencies should all use the same departmental appraisal system for their top cadres. So the second form of MBR (after the original one for the CES) was designed for that group and is the one that I showcased around the country at the request of the federal government's central personnel agency, the US Office of Personnel Management (OPM).[4] The approach had four phases.

The first was for performance planning by executives and managers with the review and approval of their superiors. In the first part of the plan, objectives were set and weighted. The total weight could range from 60 to 80 points. The second part was for setting expectations about manner of performance in eight predetermined areas (e.g., manner of planning). The areas were operationally defined by a set of behavioral examples listed on a five level-scale from more negative to more positive. Those areas applicable for the performance year were weighted, with the total allowed to range from 20 to 40 points.

The second phase involved performance monitoring by supervisors and two progress review meetings with subordinates.

In the third phase, supervisors rated their subordinates' performance, first on results, then on behaviors, using a five-level scale for both parts. A score for results and a score for manner of performance were computed by adding the products of the weights and rating levels. The two scores were then combined into a total performance score. The total score could range from zero to 400 points.[5] These scores were then put into five categories. For example, a score from 361 to 400 points was put into the "outstanding" category.

In the fourth phase, senior executives and managers were grouped into "performance areas" of similar organizational work, and bonuses and merit salary increases were distributed within these groups based on the individuals' performance scores.

For the bulk of the workforce, the "rank and file," a different tactic was taken. It was decided that each of the department's component agencies should be delegated authority over their own performance appraisal systems for the lower-level masses. But strings were attached in the form of departmental policies, which I had to write, such as the requirement that all lower-level systems must account for both behaviors and results. Without that requirement, of course, MBR would have ceased being MBR. I won't highlight the policies or the MBR off springs in the component agencies because it wouldn't serve any useful purpose here.

Commonalities Among the Earlier MBRs. Common to these earlier MBRs were their hierarchical settings with performance management from above, naturally, a legal impetus behind them, an incredible complexity, use of ratings, and no accountability for ethical behavior. Government and hierarchy, of course, go hand in hand. But without the legal impetus, the court decree driving the CES or the CSRA driving the federal civil service system, there would not have been a history of MBR for me to summarize.

As for complexity and bureaucracy, they go hand in hand, but I added some unnecessary complexity of my own doing, I'm sorry to say. As for ratings, they were required, but I didn't object because rating methodology was my forte. As for accountability for ethical behavior by any performance management process was out of the question (recall my mentioning in Chapter 8 the worst-case example set by the federal government).

Note that I didn't highlight the use of the earlier MBRs for penalizing poor performance in government. The omission is deliberate. The government lacked then and probably still does both a simple way and a resolute will to deal with poor performance when it happens.[6] The CSRA and the implementing regulations of OPM nay have even exacerbated matters. My frequent protests to the government about its safe havens for mediocrity, including "frozen PIPs" (the perpetual performance improvement plans I mentioned in Chapter 6), "dangling marginals" (a rating category that actually protected bunglers and loafers), and about an unduly long and confusing appeals process, might as well have been flatulence in a hurricane.

An Experimental MBR That Failed Positively. The final MBR of my hierarchical days was an experimental model.[7] It was motivated by my belated but finally intense desire to shed ratings forever. In just over a decade or so, performance appraisal had reverted to being a sham again. Imperial raters were having a field day fudging their ratings. Pay-for-performance had become pay-for-ratings. In some localities, more than 90% of the people were rated "outstanding." As I already mentioned, when that happens, the only people who "stand out" are the very few rated just one level lower.

A good experiment would have compared the MBR hobbled by legislative and regulatory requirements and red tape and a new MBR free of those constraints. But the government wouldn't allow it. So I designed and directed a quasi-experiment. The regular MBR was used as required. But a mock MBR was tried, too. It was a mock one in that only the regular MBR could be used for official decisions, such as pay-for-performance. The mock MBR used questions and answers instead of ratings. Supervisors answered the questions (self appraisals would have been too much of a shock) and then made mock reward decisions based on the answers. The mock MBR was much preferred by users over the regular one, and the mock reward decisions were logically defensible. I presented testimony on the successful study to a committee chartered by the Congress to consider further reforms. But the Congress wouldn't budge. I regretted that, but it made me determined to capitalize some day on that positive failure.

Section 2. Three Lessons Learned.

With all due respect, Mr. Carter, you were naïve. So was I. The S was too formidable in our performance equations. We were no match for the bureaucracy and the micromanaging by its board of 535 directors (the US Congress). Many other kinds of reforms must precede further civil service reform if there is to be any chance of taller performance by our government. That was the first lesson.

The second lesson was that performance management isn't a complex concept to understand and certainly shouldn't be a complex practice. But simplicity is impossible in a bureaucracy.

The third lesson is an old one. "If at first you don't succeed, try again." That's why I've written this book. The principles in it and the illustrative We/Me model of MBR are very sound I believe, even in a bureaucracy if it's willing to change.

NOTES AND REFERENCES FOR APPENDIX F

1. Brumback, GB. (1993). The continuing evolution of MBR and related developments. *Public Administration Review*, 53, 213-219.

2. Brumback, GB. ((1978). Toward a new theory and system of performance evaluation: A standardized MBO approach. *Public Personnel Management*, 7, 205-211.

3. Brumback, GB. (1981). Revisiting an approach to managing behaviors and results. *Public Personnel Management*, 10, 270-277.

4. Brumback, GB. (1980, January). Managing managerial performance. Invited address given at the Performance Appraisal Showcase, US Office of Personnel Management, Washington, DC.

5. Thomas S. McFee, who was also a former math teacher, conceived the scoring formula.

6. Brumback, GB. (1995). The unemployment-at-will doctrine. *Labor Law Journal*, <u>46</u>, 111-115.

7. Brumback, GB. (1993). 16 elephants can't do what a change in law could. *Public PersonnelManagement,* <u>22</u>, 237-242.

About the Author

In the course of over 50 years, the author has been affiliated with the retailing business, the manufacturing business, the not-for-profit, but extremely competitive research business, and the US government.

Dr. Brumback is the creator of the successful MBR as well as its new We/Me model, an authority on the institutionalization of ethics and on performance management, and the only author with four articles in a book of readings on the latter subject published by an international association of professionals. He has also authored numerous other articles and book reviews.

He received his Ph.D. in industrial/organizational psychology from The Ohio State University in 1963. Recognized for his achievements and contributions to his field, he was elected a fellow years ago of both The American Psychological Association and The American Psychological Society. He is also a member of the Academy of Management and of the Society for Business Ethics.